Series / Number 03-019

Complaining: Comparative Aspects of Complaint Behavior and Attitudes Toward Complaining in Canada and Britain

KARL A. FRIEDMANN
University of Calgary

 SAGE PUBLICATIONS / Beverly Hills / London

Copyright © 1974 by Sage Publications, Inc.

Printed in the United States of America

All rights reserved. No part of this book may be reproduced
or utilized in any form or by any means, electronic or mechanical,
including photocopying, recording, or by any
information storage and retrieval system, without permission in writing
from the publisher.

For information address:

SAGE PUBLICATIONS, INC.　　　　SAGE PUBLICATIONS LTD
275 South Beverly Drive　　　　　　　St George's House / 44 Hatton Garden
Beverly Hills, California 90212　　　　London EC1N 8ER

International Standard Book Number 0-8039-0454-1

Library of Congress Catalog Card No. 74-78045

FIRST PRINTING

When citing a professional paper, please use the proper form. Remember to cite the correct Sage Professional Paper series title and include the paper number. One of the two following formats can be adapted (depending on the style manual used):

(1) OSTROM, E. et al. (1973) "Community Organization and the Provision of Police Services." Sage Professional Papers in Administrative and Policy Studies, 1, 03-001. Beverly Hills and London: Sage Pubns.

OR

(2) Ostrom, Elinor, et al. 1973 *Community Organization and the Provision of Police Services.* Sage Professional Papers in Administrative and Policy Studies, vol. 1, series no. 03-001. Beverly Hills and London: Sage Publications.

CONTENTS

I. Complaining, Attitudes, and Behavior 5
II. Hypothetical Complaint Behavior 7
    Action in Case of Complaint 7
    Explaining Hypothetical Complaint Behavior 11
    Effectiveness of Channels of Complaint 15
    Channel Effectiveness Choices Compared 19
III. Attitudes Towards Complaining 24
IV. Political Efficacy 28
V. Complaint Behavior 33
    Making a Complaint 33
    Complaining and Levels of Government 35
    Choice of Channels of Complaint 39
    Evaluation of Complaint Experience 42
VI. Complaint Behavior and Attitudes 44
VII. Conclusions 57
    Notes 60
    References 63
    Appendix 64

Complaining: Comparative Aspects of Complaint Behavior and Attitudes Toward Complaining in Canada and Britain

KARL A. FRIEDMANN
University of Calgary

I. COMPLAINING, ATTITUDES, AND BEHAVIOR

Complaining is one form of interaction between the citizen and the political system. As such it has received relatively little attention.[1] Yet complaining is not a uniquely modern phenomenon: in a more general way, petitions and the redress of grievances formed an important part of politics and the process of constitutional development in Britain from the thirteenth to the nineteenth century.[2] More recently, with the democratization of political institutions, complaining has lost its constitutional significance. Being concerned only with isolated incidents of bureaupathology the subject failed to stimulate any lasting interest which partially accounts for our almost complete lack of knowledge about complaining. Even politicians who are intimately involved with complaints show an amazing lack of knowledge and sometimes clear misconceptions about the incidence of complaining,[3] although estimating the quantity of complaints should be a relatively simple task. When we consider the more complex subjects of complaint behavior and attitudes towards complaining there is even less knowledge and data to fall back on.

AUTHOR'S NOTE: *The research on which this paper is based was supported by grants from the Canada Council which are gratefully acknowledged. The computer analyses were funded by The University of Calgary. J. T. Woods (Calgary) assisted with the survey instruments. T. E. Flanagan (Calgary) developed a sampling plan for the Alberta surveys. Earlier separate draft reports on one or more of the surveys were reviewed by W. B. Gwyn (Tulane), L. B. Hill (Oklahoma), and J. T. Woods (Calgary). I am greatly indebted to them for their assistance. This paper was originally prepared for delivery at the Annual Meeting of the Canadian Political Science Association at Sir George Williams University, Montreal, in August 1973.*

As part of a more comprehensive study of Ombudsmen in Britain and Canada (more specifically Alberta) survey data were collected from samples of the British and Alberta populations to investigate their perception and evaluation of the Ombudsman.[4] Attitudes towards complaining and data on complaint behavior were peripheral to that inquiry but the results obtained—especially with the opportunity for making cross-cultural comparisons—throw some interesting light on a little-known subject that deserves more attention.

Attitudes towards complaining are part of an individual's total belief system about the political and social system in which he lives. More general and related concepts such as political efficacy and political competence have been investigated[5] but none of the handbooks on attitude scales (Robinson et al., 1969; Shaw and Wright, 1967) report a specific investigation of attitudes towards complaining. The last of the three surveys on which this discussion relies, contained a more detailed political efficacy scale which was found to reflect closely our sample's attitudes.[6] Complaining should be understood as an activity that varies with situational factors. Rokeach's (1968) concept of attitude is useful here in that he emphasizes the frequently neglected attitude towards situation, in contrast to the usual concentration on attitude towards object. This emphasis will be useful in analyzing the relationship between attitudes and behavior. He has offered the following definition of attitude: "An attitude is a relatively enduring organization of beliefs around an object or situation predisposing one to respond in some preferential manner" (1968: 450). He elaborates on three components of a belief:

(1) a cognitive component which represents a person's knowledge, held with varying degrees of certitude, about what is true or false, good or bad, etc.;

(2) an affective component: under certain conditions a belief is capable of arousing affect centering around the object of the belief itself when its validity is seriously questioned, as in an argument;

(3) a behavioral component: the belief constitutes a response predisposition. When suitably activated it must lead to some action.

As used here the term complaint behavior will refer to one or both of the following: (1) the decision to complain or not to complain (a) in general, applying to any occasion that might arise or (b) applying only to one specific occasion of perceived maladministration; (2) the actions taken, in particular the complaint channels employed, after the decision to complain has been made.

We will also use the term "hypothetical complaint behavior." The justification for its use is partly practical: available data are frequently not measurements of attitudes or measurements of actual behavior but responses to questions about hypothetical situations. In addition, attitude and behavior overlap conceptually. When we measure an attitude, especially when we aim at isolating the behavioral component of beliefs, we usually put respondents under the stimulus of a hypothetical situation. The observable response is an expression of an opinion about the likely behavior of the respondent in a certain situation or towards a certain object. It is neither behavior nor strictly an attitude, although we infer attitudes from such responses. It is therefore more useful for our purposes here to speak of "hypothetical complaint behavior."

II. HYPOTHETICAL COMPLAINT BEHAVIOR

In discussions of the relationship between the citizen and public authorities, political scientists and politicians have in the past been content to make perfunctory references to abundantly available channels of complaint: the courts of the land ensure the citizen justice, the elected representatives work for the redress of their constituents' grievances and, finally, the press of a free country throws the weight of public opinion behind an underdog harried by public officials. Usually no attention was paid to the availability of these traditional channels of complaint to people or a variety of people. During the last decade some attention was given to the adequacy and the effectiveness of these traditional channels of complaint. In some systems they were considered inadequate for a variety of reasons. The adoption of an Ombudsman became a very popular remedy. Britain and Alberta introduced an Ombudsman in 1967. In assessing complaint behavior we will also consider the usefulness and relevance of the traditional and new channels of complaint, and will pay attention to such factors as cost, availability and social appropriateness.

ACTION IN CASE OF COMPLAINT

We will first consider the following questions: (1) What proportion of the population appears willing to complain in a hypothetical case of maladministration? (2) Which channels of complaint are people aware of, or would they employ, to resolve their complaint? The first interview question was designed to give a very general impression of our sample's hypothetical behavior:

> First I would like you to think about a situation where a civil servant or a government agency had treated you unfairly. What do you think you would do about it? What would you do in such a situation?[7]

The term unfair treatment suggested a legitimate complaint. The question was intentionally kept very general and did not specify examples, or the level of government. Respondents who requested more details were asked to list all actions for all cases of complaint they could imagine. Up to four responses were coded in detailed categories. Table 1 shows the first two responses.[8]

About 60 percent of the Alberta population and 74 percent of the British population appear ready to take some definite action in case of perceived maladministration. However, a large proportion of respondents in each sample (about one quarter of all Alberta, and 16 percent of all British respondents) apparently do not know what to do in case of conflict with bureaucracy. Their responses indicate that the existing channels of complaint do not play an important role in these respondents' perception of their political environment. Another group of respondents (13 and 17 percent in Alberta; 10 percent in Britain) reported that they would not do anything in such a conflict situation. The survey did not directly probe for their reasons[9] – but cross-tabulations with socio-economic factors will allow some suggestions.

We ought to anticipate briefly one observation about this group of "Don't know" and "Do nothing" respondents. A later question showed that a fair proportion of them (14 percent, Alberta 1971; 10 percent, U.K.) had actually made a complaint at least once and used a specific channel to seek redress. This should be compared with 21 (Alberta) and 17 percent (U.K.) in the entire sample who had made a complaint.[10] We see that while these respondents were underrepresented among actual complainants, they were by no means completely absent. This observation is also valid when we consider the "Don't know" and the "Do nothing" respondents separately.[11] Their answer to the first interview question might be a genuine response error or it could be a reaction to a bad experience with actually making a complaint; the experience, of course, preceded the interview. We will return to this problem later.

Before discussing the major appeal channels (items 4 to 11 in Table 1) we should briefly comment on a lengthy list of lesser avenues for appealing administrative decisions (items 12 to 23 in Table 1). Some of these channels apparently play a much less significant role for our samples than might have been expected in the light of the importance attributed to them by politicians and interpreters of the respective constitutions. Three to four percent mention the courts and legal action; about one percent mention the news media; just over one percent mention their union or professional association; under two percent mention various forms of civic action, including the use of the ballot box. While these avenues of appeal exist we must conclude that they are quite insignificant for both the British and Alberta populations. The courts of the land apparently are not

TABLE 1

Action in Case of Complaint--First Two Responses in Two
Alberta Surveys, One U.K.--Relative Frequency Distribution

	First response			Second response		
	Alta. 1969	Alta. 1971	U.K. 1969	Alta. 1969	Alta. 1971	U.K. 1969
1. No answer	1.8	2.4	0.7	72.4	80.9	78.7
2. Don't know	24.8	20.4	15.5	1.4	2.5	0.1
3. Do nothing	12.8	16.6	9.7	0.8	1.1	0.7
4. Ombudsman	4.4	4.7	1.6	0.9	1.2	1.1
5. M.P.	11.0	7.6	23.4	2.2	1.6	6.9
6. M.L.A.	4.7	4.4	-	4.2	2.3	-
7. Alderman/Councillor	2.8	1.4	3.9	1.1	0.5	1.3
8. Minister, Premier	1.5	1.0	1.7	2.3	0.5	0.8
9. Department concerned	19.0	15.4	20.7	3.4	1.3	1.6
10. Higher level of dept.	9.7	9.5	3.5	5.0	2.1	0.8
11. Dept. Head/Dep. Min.	0.6	5.7	11.3	0.8	2.1	3.3
12. Newspaper	0.8	0.7	1.2	0.9	0.3	1.2
13. Radio or TV	0.2	0	0	0.1	0.2	0
14. Lawyer	1.8	3.4	2.4	1.1	1.4	1.6
15. Go to court	0.2	0.6	0.3	0.4	0.3	0.2
16. Complain to Union	0.3	1.0	0.9	0.1	0.3	0.3
17. Farmers' union	0	0.1	0	0.2	0	0.1
18. Professional ass'n.	0.1	0.6	0.3	0	0	0
19. Petition	1.1	0.3	0.3	0.4	0.2	0.3
20. Demonstration	0.2	0.5	0.2	0	0	0
21. Form civic ass'n.	0.3	0	0.1	0.3	0	0.1
22. Vote against govt.	0	1.0	0	0	0	0
23. Others	2.2	2.5	2.3	2.2	1.1	0.9
Totals[a]	100.3%	99.8%	100.0%	100.2%	99.9%	100.0%
(N)	(1010)	(994)	(1000)	(1010)	(994)	(1000)

[a]Percentages are reported as calculated by the computer. Totals will vary slightly from 100%.

the place where the citizen of either jurisdiction looks for administrative justice. Table 2 shows these same responses summarized in broader categories. It also contains figures from a New Zealand survey which included a comparable question.[12]

TABLE 2

Action in Case of Complaint--Surveys from Alberta, Britain and New Zealand--First Response in General Categories

	Alta. 1969	Alta. 1971	U.K. 1969	N.Z. 1966
Don't know--Do nothing	39.4	39.4	25.9	24.6
Department	29.3	30.6	35.5	33.3
Elected Representative	20.0	14.4	29.0	14.8
Ombudsman	4.4	4.7	1.6	14.0
Legal action	2.0	4.0	2.7	3.0
News Media	1.0	0.7	1.2	0.8
All others	4.2	6.0	4.1	9.5
Totals	100.3%	99.8%	100.0%	100.0%
(N)	(1010)	(994)	(1000)	(489)

The two Alberta surveys show a considerable congruity. The largest group of respondents are those who don't know what to do or who just would not complain; the second largest group are those who would go back to the administrative agency which caused the problem; the third largest group would immediately turn to their elected representative for help. New Zealand and Britain have, of course, unitary systems of government. Their citizen deals with two levels of government. Canada has a federal system and the Alberta citizen deals with three levels of government. Problems of overlapping authority and of confusion of levels of government must be greater in the case of Alberta than with the British or New Zealanders. However, in comparing the Alberta response pattern in very general categories with that of Britain and New Zealand we find a few significant differences and some interesting similarities: (1) the proportion of "Don't know" and "Do nothing" responses is considerably larger in Alberta than in Britain or New Zealand; this suggests that a larger proportion of the Alberta population than of either the British or New Zealand populations is inexperienced or politically not efficacious. (2) It appears that elected representatives play a more important role in grievance alleviation in the perception of the British population than in that of both the Alberta and New Zealand populations. (3) The proportions of respondents who turn to administrative channels, or those who turn to legal action or to the news media is strikingly similar as well as surprisingly low in all three jurisdictions. (4) One major difference may be seen in the role apparently played by the Ombudsman for the three populations. In the case of Britain the Ombudsman is not accessible to the public except through M.Ps. In New Zealand, the Ombudsman appears to have achieved a fairly prominent position as a channel of complaint, in fact, he is perceived almost as important as elected representatives there; the Alberta Ombudsman, however, does not appear to figure that prominently in the minds of the population.

EXPLAINING HYPOTHETICAL COMPLAINT BEHAVIOR

When we examine our respondents' hypothetical complaint behavior in relation to a number of demographic and other variables we notice that almost all these variables show a statistically significant association. Using Cramer's V[13] to indicate the strength of association between variables consisting of nominal data we find the following five variables significant in both the 1971 Alberta sample and the British sample in descending order of importance:

(1) political efficacy;[14]
(2) education;[15]
(3) occupation;
(4) socio-economic level;[16] and
(5) income.[17]

Tables 3A and 3B show cross-tabulations of three of these variables for both surveys.

In both samples we find that the "Don't know—Do nothing" respondents come disproportionately from the lower socio-economic levels of the population, from those with a lower level of educational attainment and from those with a low sense of political efficacy. The trend is reversed for the other categories of hypothetical complaint behavior. Respondents are more likely to use administrative appeal channels (Department) the higher up they are on the socio-economic scale, the higher their level of

TABLE 3A

Action in Case of Complaint by Socio-economic Level, Education, and Political Efficacy
Alberta, 1971

Action in case of complaint	Socio-economic level[a]			Education[b]				Political Efficacy[c] Scaled[d]		
	Below Av'ge	Av'ge	Above Av'ge	Elementary	High School	Technical	University	Low	Medium	High
Don't know--do nothing	57	39	30	62	42	27	18	61	38	24
Ombudsman	1	4	8	4	3	6	10	2	4	7
Elected Rep.	7	16	16	8	15	19	17	8	16	18
Department	26	29	37	17	29	39	43	19	29	41
Others	9	12	9	9	11	9	12	10	13	10
Totals	100%	100%	100%	100%	100%	100%	100%	100%	100%	100%
(N)	(165)	(569)	(259)	(177)	(516)	(89)	(171)	(282)	(352)	(360)

a) N = 993; $X^2p < .001$; Cramer's V = .14
b) N = 953; $X^2p < .001$; Cramer's V = .17
c) N = 994; $X^2p < .001$; Cramer's V = .22
d) See note 18

TABLE 3B

Action in Case of Complaint by Socio-economic Level, Education, and Political Efficacy--Britain

Action in case of complaint	Socio-economic level[a]			Further Education[b]		Political Efficacy Scale[e] [c]			
	Below Av'ge	Av'ge	Above Av'ge	No	Yes	Low 1	2	3	High 4
Don't know--do nothing	37	27	14	32	17	52	24	14	9
Elected Rep.	25	31	29	28	30	21	29	36	28
Department	29	33	46	32	42	19	38	40	51
Others[d]	9	9	11	8	11	8	9	10	12
Totals	100%	100%	100%	100%	100%	100%	100%	100%	100%
(N)	(258)	(466)	(274)	(599)	(374)	(217)	(411)	(270)	(102)

a) N = 998; p < .001; Cramer's V = .14
b) N = 973; p < .001; Cramer's V = .17
c) N = 1000; p < .001; Cramer's V = .20
d) The Ombudsman is not listed as a separate category in this table
e) See note 19

education, and the higher they score on the political efficacy scale. This is true too of the Ombudsman (Alberta) and political appeal channels (elected representatives) although the tendency is not as strong for the latter.

These conclusions should not be surprising. We could name a few obvious, though speculative, explanations for this hypothetical complaint behavior based on an assessment of the normal functioning of these appeal channels. The well educated person knows where to turn first, second, etc. When the more knowledgeable, articulate, and resourceful person turns to the administrative agency at which his complaint originated he will be able to communicate as part of his appeal his awareness of the availability of further recourse in case his complaint is not considered fairly. Those who use these "threats" believe that they have an effect on administrators. The poor person usually has little education, does not know of the various appeal channels or their capabilities, has no resources and few, if any, "threats" available. If he knows of any he is more likely to turn to political appeal channels in an attempt to utilize the influence of elected representatives or the press for the redress of his complaint. The data on hypothetical complaint behavior from two different populations confirm these speculations.

It is difficult on the basis of these data to go one step further and to speak of a causal relationship between education or income, etc. and hypothetical complaint behavior. We may use partial correlations to discover spurious associations. Age and sex of respondents for example, first showed a statistically significant association with hypothetical complaint behavior, but when we controlled for the effects of education or socio-economic level, age and sex were no longer statistically significant. Partial correlations may also be used—with some caution [20]—to get an indication of the relative importance of the several explanatory factors for hypothetical complaint behavior. The procedure confirmed for both samples the relative importance of the five variables as established earlier by Cramer's V, but allows us to add the following conclusion. The significance of the three economic indicators (occupation, income, socio-economic level) diminishes somewhat when we control for education and political efficacy [21] while the latter two retain their full significance when controlled for other variables or combinations of variables. The economic indicators remain statistically significant but education and sense of political efficacy appear as the major explanatory factors for the hypothetical complaint behavior of our respondents in both Alberta and Britain.

EFFECTIVENESS OF CHANNELS OF COMPLAINT

The main purpose of the first interview question was to get an impression of what type of action respondents would take in a hypothetical complaint situation. Several considerations may be involved in the response obtained: (1) immediate awareness of a particular channel; (2) the propriety of using a particular channel first, another next and yet another one as a last resort as well as considerations concerned with the level of government; (3) the effectiveness of a particular channel in achieving results quickly, cheaply, etc. However, a more direct measurement of the samples' perception of the effectiveness of specific channels of complaint appeared desirable. The aggregate ratings obtained can be used also as an indication of the hypothetical complaint behavior of our samples under the assumption that in an actual complaint situation the respondent would sooner or later resort to that channel which he considered most effective.

To obtain such effectiveness choices for all channels respondents were handed a page listing nine of them; respondents were asked to read the list and then to name "the best or most effective means of raising a complaint against a government department" ("a provincial government department in Alberta"). They were then asked whether they considered others on this list effective, and up to two responses were coded in the sequence in which they were offered. Respondents were also asked to name from the same list the most effective means of raising a complaint about a federal government department (Alberta samples only), and finally a complaint about local government. Tables 4A and 4B show the responses obtained.[22]

We will first compare the responses in the two Alberta surveys with each other. If we look at the frequency with which provincial government departments were chosen, we find them ranking first in 1969 with an impressive score of 34 percent, nearly twice as high as the channel ranking second, the member of the provincial legislature (MLA). In 1971, the department attracted only half as many choices and ranks second, only 1 percent higher than the channel ranked third (Minister).

The Member of the Legislative Assembly ranks second in 1969 and first in 1971 with one quarter of all choices, an increase of about 6 percent over 1969. Ministers play a dual role as heads of departments and as elected representatives. The latter role should be expected to dominate the role perception that our respondents have of Ministers. Ministers rank only fifth in 1969 with little more than 5 percent of all choices, but third in 1971, tripling the 1969 score.

TABLE 4A

Effectiveness Choices for Channels of Complaint--Three Levels of Government--Alberta 1969 and 1971

	Provincial Complaints						Federal Complaints				Local Govt. Complaints	
	Most effect.		Other effect.(1)		Other effect.(2)		Most effect.				Most effect.	
	1969	1971	1969	1971	1969	1971	1969	1971	1969	1971	1969	1971
1. Complain to the government dept. concerned	34.1	17.4	1.0	14.0	0.4	1.9	19.0	14.0			12.5	4.4
2. Write to a newspaper	9.0	6.9	3.1	10.0	0.2	2.3	3.5	3.0			4.5	7.1
3. Write to or phone radio or TV station	4.3	4.8	4.2	6.9	1.0	2.3	1.2	2.4			1.6	3.6
4. Ask your union or professional ass'n for help	5.1	4.3	3.3	4.1	0.4	1.6	2.7	3.1			1.4	1.1
5. Write to or talk to your M.P.	9.0	13.5	4.8	6.8	0.7	1.3	43.7	44.8			1.5	2.3
6. Write to or talk to your M.L.A.	18.6	24.8	17.2	16.0	3.3	3.9	4.3	5.7			2.1	4.8
7. Take it to your Alderman or Councillor or Mayor	2.0	2.8	2.4	4.1	1.5	1.1	1.0	1.3			59.3	65.2
8. Take it to a lawyer	2.2	4.5	4.0	5.2	1.7	0.9	1.7	1.7			1.8	2.5
9. Write to the minister concerned	5.5	16.3	12.5	17.9	7.1	4.7	8.5	14.3			1.2	2.2
No answer (or none effective)	10.2	4.7	47.5	15.0	83.7	80.0	14.4	9.7			14.1	6.8
Totals[a]	100%	100%	100%	100%	100%	100%	100%	100%			100%	100%

a) See note 23

TABLE 4B

Effectiveness Choices for Channels of Complaint--Two Levels of Government--Britain

	Most effective		Other effective (1)		Other effective (2)	
	Central Govt.	Local Govt.	Central Govt.	Local Govt.	Central Govt.	Local Govt.
1. Complain to Govt. Dept. (or local authority) concerned	20.5	14.9	8.4	5.6	2.0	0.7
2. Write to a newspaper	21.7	12.1	16.8	10.2	4.0	1.1
3. Write to (or phone) radio or TV station	2.6	0.5	3.9	1.3	1.5	0.2
4. Ask your Union (or professional association) for help	4.2	0.5	7.2	1.2	1.6	0.3
5. Write to your MP or talk to him	25.7	10.9	19.7	4.4	4.2	0.8
6. Take it to your Alderman or Councillor	2.8	42.7	3.3	10.6	1.7	0.5
7. Take it to the Citizens' Advice Bureau	5.3	4.9	6.4	4.3	2.6	0.5
8. Take it to a lawyer or go to a Court	3.7	2.1	6.5	3.1	1.7	1.1
9. Write to the Minister concerned	9.1	1.5	8.2	0.8	3.5	0
No answer (or none effective)	4.4	9.9	19.6	58.5	77.2	94.8
Totals	100%	100%	100%	100%	100%	100%

[17]

Members of Parliament share the third rank with newspapers in 1969, with a score of 9 percent each. Federal MPs increased their score to 13 percent and rank fourth in 1971. The M.P. is of course, in this case, the inappropriate elected representative; the question asked for effectiveness choices for provincial complaints. While we may assume that some respondents confused the M.P. with the M.L.A., we also know that some M.P.s who are well known in their federal constituencies are approached for help with strictly provincial complaints. We cannot be sure to what extent the scores represent respondents' perception of the latter role.

Among the other channels offered, newspapers rank relatively high, fourth (1969) and fifth (1971). The news media, in general, rank third after the political and bureaucratic appeal channels, scoring better than legal remedies and interest groups.

This particular interview question produced the only major difference in the response pattern between the 1969 and the 1971 Alberta surveys. We may be dealing with a genuine attitude change over a period of time between the two surveys: provincial departments may have lost in credibility what M.L.A.s and Ministers gained. Yet the magnitude of the change is quite considerable: attitudes don't normally change that fast that much; at least we can say that about attitudes which are central to political belief systems. However, attitudes towards channels of complaint or their effectiveness are probably marginal to most political belief systems, and might therefore fluctuate more easily. If we look for factors which might have contributed to such a fluctuation, we notice that the 1971 survey was taken in February, 1971, with a provincial election being expected any time within two to six months; it was eventually held in August, 1971, and brought a change of government, the first such change since 1935. The Alberta scene in February, 1971, was more obviously political than two years earlier. M.L.A.s and Ministers were definitely more visible, perhaps actually more active. This highly political atmosphere in February, 1971 may have contributed to a higher rating of the effectiveness of political channels of complaint (M.L.A., Minister) and the corresponding decrease in the rating of bureaucratic (department) and other, less obviously political channels. The 1971 election situation may not completely explain the magnitude of the differing response pattern. With 90 and 95 percent of the sample giving an effectiveness choice we may assume that some of them responded to the stimulus of having a list with enumerated items in front of them, who might otherwise not have expressed an opinion; given the expectation expressed above concerning attitudes that are marginal to a political belief system, we also have to expect greater variation in recorded opinions.

Table 4B shows the detailed effectiveness choices obtained from our British sample. Whether we look at the first response alone or at the first and second response simultaneously, we see the following rank ordering for complaint channels against central government departments: the M.P. ranks highest, followed closely by newspapers; the appeal to the department ranks third and the Minister fourth. This ranking of channels differs significantly from the frequency with which these channels were mentioned in response to the first question. The very high ranking of newspapers in particular came as a surprise.

In Table 3B we also reported British effectiveness choices for methods of complaining against local government. Again, the appropriate elected representative (Alderman, Councillor) is rated highest—in fact, higher than the next three together—the local government department ranks second, newspapers third (with an additional very high second response rating) and the MP ranks fourth. The very high rating of the Councillor/Alderman must surprise. We know that MPs are frequently asked to help with local government complaints, and the fact that 11 percent of the sample consider the MP as the most effective channel of complaint about local government should confirm both their involvement and their perceived success in the role.[24] Many MPs consider that they have to look after many more complaints about local government than about central government.[25]

CHANNEL EFFECTIVENESS CHOICES COMPARED

To facilitate comparisons between the Alberta and the British response pattern of effectiveness choices we have listed the first response in Table 5 in a slightly adjusted form.

The following general conclusions may be offered: (1) With only one exception we find in each sample in Alberta and Britain the appropriate elected representative at all levels of government receiving the highest proportion of effectiveness choices. This preeminent position of the elected representative as the highest ranked channel of complaint is enhanced if we consider the aggregate of all references to elected representatives—whether appropriate, formally speaking, or not appropriate for the level of government. (2) Returning to the department which caused the complaint attracts the second highest number of effectiveness choices in Alberta, while in Britain the news media, especially newspapers, rank somewhat higher than Departments as effective complaint channels. (3) The Minister as a grievance channel is more difficult to rank and fluctuates

TABLE 5

Effectiveness Choices for Channels of Complaint--Alberta and Britain (First Response)

	Provincial complaints Alberta		National (Fed.) complaints Alberta				Local govt. complaints Alberta			
	1969	1971	1969	1971	Britain 1969		1969	1971	Britain 1969	
1. Department	34	17	19	14	21		13	5	15	
2. Minister	6	16	9	14	9		1	2	1	
3. Elected rep. (appropriate for level)	19	25	44	45	26		59	65	43	
4. Elected rep. (from other levels of govt.)	11	16	5	7	3		4	7	11	
5. Media	13	12	5	5	24		6	11	13	
6. All others	7	9	4	5	13		3	4	7	
7. No answer (or none effective)	10	5	14	10	4		14	6	10	
Totals	100%	100%	100%	100%	100%		100%	100%	100%	

by sample and level of government in the case of Alberta. He must generally, however, be considered as the third most important channel before the news media which would rank fourth. In Britain the Minister ranks fourth. We find as the greatest difference between Britain and Alberta the high effectiveness attributed to newspapers in the U.K., and as a second difference Albertans' greater confidence in government departments as effective redressers of grievances.

If we check effectiveness choices against a number of demographic variables, the most surprising finding is negative; the ratings are not associated with the level of education in any sample. We find some association with the socio-economic level of respondents and with occupation. Table 6 shows a selection from each sample. The observable trends in the effectiveness attributed to channels are similar to those already reported in the discussion of hypothetical complaint behavior (with the noted exception of education) although these trends are not as strong as might be expected. There is no apparent explanation for the absence of a significant association between channel effectiveness choice and education. Respondents' score on the political efficacy scale, on the other hand, does show a very strong association with channel effectiveness choices for all three samples. Table 7 shows three examples. The higher a respondent scored on political efficacy the more likely was he to choose the department or the appropriate elected representative as the most effective channel. And the lower his political efficacy score the more likely was he to choose the news media or other channels (interest group, law). The trend is fairly consistent over all levels of government, though not quite as strong for the federal (Alberta only) and local levels (not shown in Table 7), for three channels involved: the department, the elected representative (appropriate for the respective level of government), and the news media. In general the elected representative takes somewhat of a middle position between the department and the media; although chosen more frequently by respondents with higher political efficacy scores than by those with lower scores, the difference is not as large as in the case of the department and the media. Again, this trend is easy to appreciate: a person with a low sense of political efficacy is attracted to the power of the media, which might be harnessed for his case in view of his self-assessed powerlessness. On the other side we find the person with a high sense of political efficacy choosing the more appropriate channels (department; elected representative) and having the confidence that he can effect a proper hearing of his case.

TABLE 6

Effectiveness Choices for Channels of Complaint--Alberta 1969 by Income; Alberta 1971 by Socio-economic Level; Britain by Occupation

	Alberta (Provincial complaints) 1969[a] Income					Alberta 1971[b] Socio-econ. level			Britain (National complaints) 1969[c] Occupation			
	Under $3,000	$3,000 $5,000	$5,000 $7,500	$7,500 $10,000	Over $10,000	Below Av'ge	Av'ge	Above Av'ge	House-wife, others	Manual workers	Clerical	Exec., Professional
1. Department	27	32	31	36	44	13	17	20	17	19	21	26
2. Minister	2	4	7	8	10	15	16	19	10	10	6	11
3. Elected rep. (approp.)	18	24	19	18	16	10	28	27	28	20	27	28
4. Elected rep. (other)	8	10	13	12	9	21	15	16	2	3	4	2
5. Media	11	13	15	13	12	18	11	9	24	28	27	18
6. Others	8	7	8	8	5	10	9	7	15	14	10	13
7. No answer (or none)	26	10	7	5	4	13	4	2	4	6	5	2
Totals	100%	100%	100%	100%	100%	100%	100%	100%	100%	100%	100%	100%
(N)	(129)	(204)	(245)	(132)	(112)	(165)	(569)	(259)	(292)	(283)	(190)	(235)

a) $N = 822$; $X^2 p < .001$; Cramer's $V = .13$
b) $N = 993$; $X^2 p < .001$; Cramer's $V = .13$
c) $N = 1000$; $X^2 p = .04$; Cramer's $V = .10$

TABLE 7

Effectiveness Choices for Channels of Complaint for Two Levels of Government: Alberta 1971 and Britain (Central Government) by Political Efficacy

	Alberta						Britain					
	Provincial complaints[a]			Federal complaints[b]			Central govt. complaints[c]			Political efficacy[d]		
	Political efficacy			Political efficacy			Political efficacy					
	Low	Medium	High	Low	Medium	High	Low	Low-Med.	Med.-High	High		
1. Department	13	16	24	17	14	16	10	20	27	35		
2. Minister	19	16	17	19	17	13	8	11	9	8		
3. Elected rep. (approp.)	16	27	32	38	46	60	23	26	29	31		
4. Elected rep. (other) level of govt.	17	20	15	7	10	6	-	-	-	-		
5. Media	22	13	5	9	8	2	39	27	18	11		
6. All others	13	8	7	10	5	3	20	16	17	15		
Totals	100%	100%	100%	100%	100%	100%	100%	100%	100%	100%		
(N)	(248)	(341)	(358)	(222)	(325)	(351)	(192)	(398)	(267)	(99)		

a) $N = 947$; $X^2 p < .001$; Cramer's $V = 0.19$
b) $N = 898$; $X^2 p < .001$; Cramer's $V = 0.17$
c) $N = 956$; $X^2 p < .001$; Cramer's $V = 0.14$
d) See also note 30

[23]

III. ATTITUDES TOWARDS COMPLAINING

We expect that an individual's attitude towards complaining will be affected by the following factors: (1) personality characteristics; (2) his social and economic situation; (3) his level of confidence in the political system or generally his other attitudes towards the political system, as well as his attitudes towards various situations in which complaining occurs; and (4) his actual experience in interacting with the political system, specifically, perhaps, his actual experience with complaining. The influence of personality factors is difficult to assess with surveys of the type used in this study. The surveys do, however, include data on the socioeconomic situation of respondents and on complaint experience; in addition, the 1971 Alberta survey contained a more extensive measurement of political efficacy. The association of these factors with attitudes towards complaining will be considered below.

In the absence of a validated scale, it was assumed that attitudes towards complaining could best be ascertained by asking respondents (early in the interview) directly: "Do you feel there is any use in complaining?" Table 8 shows the response distributions.

TABLE 8

Any Use in Complaining?

	Alberta 1969	Alberta 1971	Britain 1969
Yes	46.1	49.8	45.9
No	29.6	24.3	27.7
Depends	19.2	21.3	21.4
Don't know (N.A.)	5.1	4.6	5.0
Totals	100.0%	100.0%	100.0%

About one half or just under one half of the respondents in all three samples believe in the usefulness of complaining and about one fifth of the respondents state "it depends" on a variety of factors, while about one quarter of the respondents, however, believe complaining to be a futile exercise. The similarity of the British and Alberta responses in all categories must be seen as quite remarkable. They are almost identical.

The very sizeable "Depends" response directs our attention to the complex of attitudes towards situation which interact with the attitude towards complaining. Variables of the situation in which complaints occur may be reduced to four general categories:

(1) the nature of the complaint (whether it is considered legitimate or not);
(2) the characteristics of the complainant, his personality, status, resources, etc.;
(3) the characteristics of the complaint channel and the addressee of the complaint; and
(4) the characteristics of the administrative and governmental system; the level of government; the closeness of an election, etc.

An attitude towards one or more of these situational factors will interact with a respondent's attitude towards complaining to produce the "Depends" response predisposition. The person who is aware of these situational factors is less likely to have a clear and simple positive or negative attitude towards complaining.

Cross-tabulations confirm our expectation that attitudes towards complaining are strongly associated with a number of demographic variables: income, occupation, socio-economic level, and education; a selection is shown in Tables 9A and 9B. The lower the socio-economic level of the respondent the less likely is he to have confidence in the usefulness of complaining; with increasing income levels that confidence increases, too. Among the demographic variables education shows the strongest association with this attitude in both the British and Alberta surveys. The higher the level of educational attainment the greater apparently a respondent's confidence in the usefulness of complaining.[26] A third factor, however, showed an even stronger association with attitudes towards complaining in the 1971 Alberta sample: a political efficacy scale[27] shown in Table 10.

The higher a respondent scored on political efficacy the more likely was he to believe in the usefulness of complaining. The association of these factors is very strong. The attitude response itself may well be a measure of a respondent's political efficacy. The strength of the association, as well

TABLE 9A

Usefulness of Complaining by Income-Alberta 1969, Socio-economic Level and Education-- Alberta 1971

Any use in complaining	Income (1969)[a]				Socio-econ. level (1971)[b]			Education (1971)[c]			
	Under $3,000	$3,000 $5,000	$5,000 $7,500	$7,500 $10,000	Over $10,000	Below Average	Average	Above Average	Elementary	High School	Technical	University
Yes	28	45	51	60	63	30	49	64	35	47	55	71
Depends	24	21	23	16	17	33	26	21	30	27	28	16
No	48	34	26	24	20	37	25	15	35	26	17	13
Totals	100%	100%	100%	100%	100%	100%	100%	100%	100%	100%	100%	100%
(N)	(115)	(194)	(233)	(128)	(110)	(164)	(568)	(258)	(175)	(515)	(89)	(171)

a) $N = 780$; $X^2 p < .001$; Cramer's $V = 0.15$
b) $N = 990$; $X^2 p < .001$; Cramer's $V = 0.15$
c) $N = 950$; $X^2 p < .001$; Cramer's $V = 0.16$

TABLE 9B

Usefulness of Complaining by Education, Occupation, and Single Political Efficacy Item--Britain

Any use in complaining	Education (school leaving age)[a]				Occupation[b]			Politics complicated[c]		
	14 years or less	15 years	16 years	17 years	18 years or more	Manual worker	Clerical	Exec. Professional	Agree	Don't know	Disagree
Yes	42	45	57	55	59	44	45	60	42	53	63
Depends	21	25	22	16	25	19	28	18	22	33	21
No	37	30	21	29	16	37	27	22	36	14	16
Totals	100%	100%	100%	100%	100%	100%	100%	100%	100%	100%	100%
(N)	(332)	(236)	(178)	(95)	(98)	(275)	(180)	(232)	(627)	(43)	(273)

a) $N = 939$; $X^2 p < .001$; Cramer's $V = .12$
b) $N = 687$; $X^2 p < .001$; Cramer's $V = .12$
c) $N = 943$; $X^2 p < .001$; Cramer's $V = .15$

[27]

TABLE 10

Usefulness of Complaining by Political Efficacy--
Alberta 1971

	Political Efficacy[a]				
Any use in complaining	Low 1	2	3	4	High 5
Yes	24	35	55	68	73
Depends	28	33	27	20	18
No	48	32	18	12	9
Totals	100%	100%	100%	100%	100%
(N)	(220)	(194)	(196)	(187)	(197)

a) The scale used here is Scale C as identified in Table 12.
$N = 994$; $X^2_p < .001$; Cramer's $V = .29$; Kendall's tau $c = .36$

as the logical affinity between the question on the usefulness of complaining and the items that form the basis of the political efficacy scale, led to the decision to include the former as part of the latter for the 1971 Alberta survey. Part three of Table 9B showed for the British sample a cross-tabulation between attitude towards complaining and one single political efficacy item. While one item is no substitute for a full scale, the cross-tabulation and its statistics will indicate that the relationship between complaint attitude and political efficacy is probably also valid for our British sample.

IV. POLITICAL EFFICACY

At this stage, it is necessary to discuss the political efficacy scale developed for the last Alberta survey (1971). It became clear that several subjects examined by the 1969 surveys were only partially explainable through correlation with demographic variables. Other explanatory factors might be as important or even more important. It was desirable to examine an individual's overall relationship with the political and social system. The concept of political efficacy aims at measuring one element of this relationship. Attempts to measure a "sense of political efficacy" or "political self-confidence" or "personal optimism" and "political pessimism" have been made repeatedly, often using identical items as a base for a scale.[28] Recent attempts by Dutch researchers have led to a reassessment of the usefulness of the political efficacy scale and to a broadening of the base of the scale (Mokken, 1969). Table 11 shows the eight scale items utilized in the 1971 Alberta survey; six are identical with six of nine items in Mokken's "Dutch Efficacy Scale," and two were added (items 1 and 7). A Guttman scale analysis was performed on all items and on various combinations of items. Table 12 shows inter-item and item-scale correlation coefficients. The choice for a usable political efficacy scale was reduced to three alternative scales: Scale A consisting of all eight items had the advantage of containing a large number of items, but showed unacceptably low statistics for a Guttman scale. Scales B and C had relatively small numbers of items but came close to being acceptable Guttman scales.[29] Scale C has been used in our analysis once only (Table 10) and will be used once more (Table 22). Scale A will not be used. The "Political Efficacy Scale" chosen for discussing the 1971 survey results is Scale B. It includes, with four well-tried statements, our question on the usefulness of complaining. The scale has a good structure and is of medium strength but is not a Guttman scale.[30]

This political efficacy scale shows a fairly strong association with a number of demographic variables. Table 13 presents cross-tabulations with education and socio-economic level. The political efficacy scale and most of the demographic variables represent ordinal scales. An appropriate statistical measure for the strength of association between the scale and our variables is Kendall's tau c rank order correlation coefficient. The following values for this coefficient were obtained:

Education	0.22
Socio-economic level	0.18
Occupation	0.14
Income	0.13

The level of educational attainment appears as the strongest factor in explaining political efficacy scores; socio-economic indicators play an important secondary role. This result is not surprising. Most of the recent attitude research has pointed to education as the primary explanatory factor.

TABLE 11

Political Efficacy Scale Items--Response Distributions
in Per Cent of Total Sample--Alberta 1971

	Agree	Disagree	Don't Know (NA)
1. "Any use in complaining?" ("Yes" = Agree; "No" = Disagree; "Depends," "NA" = Don't know) (Positive alternative: "Yes" and "Depends")	49.8	24.3	25.9
2. "People like me don't have any say about what the government does" (Positive alternative: "disagree")	39.0	55.9	5.0
3. "The political parties are only interested in my vote and not in my opinion" (Positive alternative: "disagree")	50.1	38.6	11.3
4. "Sometimes politics and government seem so complicated that a person like me can't really understand what's going on" (Positive alternative: "disagree")	70.7	26.7	2.6
5. "Cabinet Ministers don't care much about the opinions of people like me" (Positive alternative: "disagree")	39.2	45.0	15.8
6. "In the determination of government policy the votes of people like me are taken into account" (Positive alternative: "agree")	65.6	22.4	12.0
7. "I don't think civil servants care much about what a person like me thinks" (Positive alternative: "disagree")	42.5	44.5	13.0
8. "Members of the Legislature don't care much about the opinions of people like me" (Positive alternative: "disagree")	33.2	55.1	11.7

TABLE 12

Political Efficacy Scales--Correlation Coefficients of
Scale Items and Part-whole Correlations--Alberta 1971

	Items	1	2	3	4	5	6	7	8
1	Use in complaining	1.00							
2	No say over government action	.30	1.00						
3	Parties interested in vote	.21	.35	1.00					
4	Politics complicated	.13	.26	.11	1.00				
5	Cabinet ministers don't care	.20	.31	.36	.15	1.00			
6	Votes are considered	.13	.24	.22	.06	.21	1.00		
7	Civil servants don't care	.14	.18	.25	.07	.27	.18	1.00	
8	MLAs don't care	.23	.38	.38	.16	.39	.26	.35	1.00
	Part-whole correlation:								
	Scale A (all 8 items)	.32	.51	.48	.23	.47	.32	.35	.54
	Scale B (items 1,2,3,5,8)	.32	.49	.48	-	.46	-	-	.51
	Scale C (items 2,3,5,8)	-	.45	.48	-	.46	-	-	.51

Scale A R = .75 S = .39   (R = Coefficient of Reproducibility
Scale B R = .82 S = .55   S = Coefficient of Scalability)
Scale C R = .81 S = .57

We expected attitudes towards complaining to be affected by (1) personality factors—which we were unable to investigate, (2) by socio-economic factors—which we were able to examine and confirm, and (3) by other attitudes towards the political system. Our conclusion on this point must be that attitudes towards complaining are predominantly associated with respondents' sense of political efficacy, so much, in fact, that the question on the usefulness of complaining can well be included in the base of the political efficacy scale as one item among others measuring the same phenomenon. Attitudes towards complaining are part of an individual's general relationship to the political system; part of this relationship is assessed by the concept of political efficacy. A fourth factor, interaction with the political system or specifically actual complaint experience, might also be expected to influence a person's attitudes towards complaining. We will return to this question below.

TABLE 13

Political Efficacy Scale by Education and Socio-economic Level--Alberta 1971

Political Efficacy Scale		Education[a]					Socio-economic Level[b]		
	Elementary	Some High School	High School	Technical	Some University	University and grad.	Below Average	Average	Above Average
Low 1	19	13	8	3	7	4	22	11	3
2	25	19	15	19	13	10	25	16	16
3	22	20	17	15	10	11	16	18	15
4	19	18	19	21	18	14	19	19	19
5	10	17	20	16	23	23	11	19	20
High 6	5	13	21	26	29	38	7	17	27
Totals	100%	100%	100%	100%	100%	100%	100%	100%	100%
(N)	(177)	(318)	(198)	(89)	(90)	(81)	(165)	(569)	(259)

a) N = 953
b) N = 993

V. COMPLAINT BEHAVIOR

As indicated earlier the term complaint behavior will refer (1) to the decision to complain or not to complain (a) in general or (b) in a specific case; and (2) to the actions taken in lodging a complaint.

The earlier discussion of hypothetical complaint behavior showed that some respondents (between 10 and 16 percent) were quite determined not to complain even if they were treated unfairly by administrators. But we also noticed that at least some of these very respondents had made a complaint at least once. That alone should caution us against drawing too many inferences about actual behavior from reported hypothetical complaint behavior. The problem is, of course, not new. Almond and Verba (1963: 184-187) tried to get around it by asking their respondents how likely it would be that they would actually do something about a problem. But that will not produce more certainty about actual behavior since it merely adds a second hypothetical situation. We therefore tried, in our surveys, to get some data about the actual complaint behavior of the respondents in our samples. The interviews included a number of questions about several aspects of complaint behavior:

(1) what proportion of the sample had actually made a complaint,
(2) what level of government was involved,
(3) what channels of complaint were actually used, and
(4) how these complainants were satisfied with the replies they received.

MAKING A COMPLAINT

Respondents were first asked: "Have you ever been in a situation where you made a complaint about a civil servant or some administrative decision?" The responses are listed in Table 14.

The proportion of respondents who report having made a complaint is surprisingly small. It is a matter of speculation why only such a small proportion of people report ever having made a complaint.[31] Most likely the incidence of complaining is somewhat higher than reported by our respondents.[32] One obvious impediment to accurate reporting is the fact that memories, especially memories of unpleasant events, are short. Even if we assume that the time within immediate recollection is probably not more than two years, the proportion of respondents who have actually complained is still quite small. A less tangible psychological barrier to accurate reporting may be respondents' reluctance to appear as complainers or malcontents. This impression could be gained from reports by

TABLE 14

Ever Made a Complaint?--Relative Frequency Distributions-
Alberta and Britain

Ever made a complaint?	Alberta 1969	Alberta 1971	Britain 1969
Yes	15.0	21.0	16.6
No	83.8	78.3	80.8
No answer	1.2	0.7	2.6
Totals	100%	100%	100%

interviewers that some respondents claimed with pride: "I never complain"; other remarks reported were: "The squeaky wheels get the grease," suggesting both that the noisiest, and therefore the most unpleasant fellows get excessive attention, and that there may be quite an injustice to the rest of the quiet and good people in the special efforts made to accommodate the "complainers."[33]

All three surveys show relatively low levels of complaining for both Alberta and Britain. A. Mitchell (1968: 22) reports that about 12 percent of his sample in New Zealand had actually done something about unfair treatment by a government department. When reporting their hypothetical complaint behavior, only 10 to 17 percent of respondents stated that they would remain inactive in case of conflict with bureaucracy, but some 60 percent (Alberta) and 74 percent (U.K.) mentioned some definite action. There are, of course, many reasons why people do not actually complain: some simply do not have occasion or cause to complain; some may not want to complain, as, for example, those respondents who were so happy to be in Canada that they would never complain; some may believe they lack the knowledge, skills, and resources required to be successful; some may calculate quite rationally that the possible benefits of complaining are not worth the effort they have to make; others, again, may be held back by simple inertia. But it is impossible even to speculate about the proportion of respondents who had real cause for complaining and did, in fact, decide not to take any action. The data in our surveys suggest some partial explanations of actual complaint behavior, specifically the decision to complain or not to complain. These suggestions are all based on the assumption that the occurrence of maladministration is not itself associated with the socio-economic status or the level of education, etc. of the consumer of government services.

Cross-tabulations with demographic variables—Tables 15A to 15C—produce a fairly clear indication that socio-economic factors are associated with the decision to complain. The higher a respondent was rated on the socio-economic scale the more likely he was to report having made a complaint. Education shows a stronger association with complaining for the Alberta sample, but not for the British sample. For the latter, all three economic variables have a stronger association with complaining than education.[34] We also observe that in all three samples relatively more men than women report having made a complaint.[35]

COMPLAINING AND LEVELS OF GOVERNMENT

The respondents who reported having made a complaint were also asked what level of government was involved. Table 16 has the response distributions.

In all three samples, each level of government involved received about an equal share of all complaints. Cross-tabulations do not reveal any definitive pattern of specific groups complaining more to a specific level of government. A few points may be mentioned as suggestions, with no claim for statistical significance. The 1971 Alberta sample showed a tendency for native Albertans to complain more to the provincial level of government; for those born elsewhere in Canada to complain more to the federal government; for those born outside Canada to complain more often to the local government level. Although this particular cross-tabulation shows a statistically significant association between nativity and level of government[36] to which respondents complained, it would involve a lot of speculation to establish a causal connection. Farmers tend to complain more to the federal government. In the metropolitan areas (Calgary and Edmonton) complaints at the local government level are relatively more important.

For the British sample we observe an association between the income level and the level of government to which our respondents complained: the higher the level of income of a respondent the more likely was he to complain to the central government.[37] An observation which allows some speculation about the nature of the complaint emerged from a cross-tabulation with the housing situation of respondents: 71 percent of complainants who rented Council-owned housing had complained to the local government, while those who rented privately or were owner-occupiers complained evenly to both levels of government.

TABLE 15A

Made Complaint by Occupation and Income--Alberta 1969

Ever made a complaint?	Occupation[a]					Income[b]			
	Housewife	Man. worker	Clerical	Farmer	Exec. Professional	Under $3,000	$3,000–$5,000	$5,000–$7,500	$7,500–$10,000	Over $10,000
Yes	12	11	21	19	28	15	14	10	19	31
No	88	89	79	81	72	85	86	90	81	69
Totals	100%	100%	100%	100%	100%	100%	100%	100%	100%	100%
(N)	(335)	(93)	(492)	(139)	(127)	(129)	(203)	(243)	(129)	(109)

a) $N = 904$; $X^2 p < .001$; Cramer's $V = .12$
b) $N = 813$; $X^2 p < .001$; Cramer's $V = .15$

TABLE 15B

Made Complaint by Socio-economic Level and Education--Alberta 1971

Ever made a complaint?	Socio-economic level[a]						Education completed[b]				
	Much Below Average	Below Average	Average	Above Average	Much Above Average	Elementary	Some High School	High School Completed	Technical College	Some University	University and Grad.
Yes	12	14	20	26	40	18	15	18	24	32	42
No	88	86	80	74	60	82	84	82	76	68	58
Totals	100%	100%	100%	100%	100%	100%	100%	100%	100%	100%	100%
(N)	(17)	(146)	(567)	(219)	(37)	(177)	(316)	(196)	(88)	(90)	(79)

a) N = 986 X^2 p < .001 Cramer's V = .11

b) N = 946 X^2 p < .001 Cramer's V = .19

TABLE 15C

Made Complaint by Income, Socio-economic Level, and Education--Britain

Ever made a complaint?	Income (annual)[a]				Socio-economic level[b]			Education (school leaving age)[c]			
	£519 or less	£520-729	£730-1249	£1250-2019	£2020 or more	Below Av'ge	Av'ge	Above Av'ge	14 years or less	15 years	16 years	17 years	18 years or more
Yes	10	20	18	23	33	9	16	26	13	17	17	25	27
No	90	80	82	77	67	91	84	74	87	83	83	75	73
Totals	100%	100%	100%	100%	100%	100%	100%	100%	100%	100%	100%	100%	100%
(N)	(143)	(99)	(247)	(138)	(67)	(253)	(456)	(265)	(346)	(244)	(179)	(98)	(97)

a) $N = 694$; $X^2 p < .001$; Cramer's $V = .15$

b) $N = 974$; $X^2 p < .001$; Cramer's $V = .16$

c) $N = 964$; $X^2 p < .001$; Cramer's $V = .12$

TABLE 16

Complaint About National (Fed.), Provincial or Local Government—Actual Complainants—Alberta and Britain

	Alberta 1969	Alberta 1971	Britain 1969
National (Fed.) government	32	34	49
Provincial government	28	33	–
Local government	40	33	51
Totals	100%	100%	100%
(N)	(151)	(211)	(166)

CHOICE OF CHANNELS OF COMPLAINT

Those respondents who reported having made a complaint were asked: "What did you do about your complaint? Who did you complain to?" Responses were coded in the same detail as the hypothetical complaint behavior, but we will consider them only in general terms as listed in Table 17.

We notice immediately that a very high proportion of complainants first turned to the department with their complaint: about half the Alberta complainants and three quarters of the British. Only a small proportion of British complainants (15 percent) went immediately to their elected representative, while we find that a quarter to one third of Alberta complainants had done that. Only between 18 and 29 percent of complainants utilized a second channel. In comparing this complaint behavior with the hypothetical complaint behavior of the respective total sample we gain the general impression either that actual complainants are not representative of the entire sample in their choice of channels or that the actual complaint behavior differs significantly from the reported hypothetical complaint behavior in that more respondents will first appeal to the department. These are hazardous comparisons for a number of reasons, the most obvious being the large contingent of "Don't know—Do nothing"

TABLE 17

Channels of Complaint Used by Actual Complainants--Alberta and Britain

Complained to:	First:			Second:		
	Alta. 1969	Alta. 1971	Britain 1969	Alta. 1969	Alta. 1971	Britain 1969
Department	53	49	73	5	10	7
Elected rep.	26	32	15	8	10	5
Ombudsman	2	1	–	1	1	1
Others	19	18	12	9	8	5
N.A.	–	–	–	77	71	82
Totals	100%	100%	100%	100%	100%	100%
(N)	(151)	(211)	(166)	(151)	(211)	(166)

responses to the first question. We will therefore narrow down the comparison between hypothetical and actual complaint behavior by excluding all those for whom we do not have data on actual behavior. Table 18A allows a comparison between complainants' hypothetical and actual choice of channel of complaint for the 1971 Alberta sample.[38] Table 18B presents the same comparison for the British sample. Table 18A shows 211 complainants for the 1971 Alberta sample: (1) 54 (or one quarter) of all complainants had responded "Don't know—Do nothing" when asked for their hypothetical complaint behavior. Each of them took some action in the real complaint situation: 15 (or 28 percent) of them approached their elected representative; 24 (or 44 percent) returned to the department involved; 15 (or 28 percent) used some other channel. (2) 39 (or 18.5 percent) of all complainants named their elected representative as their choice of channel in the hypothetical situation; 24 (or 62 percent) actually chose that avenue of appeal for their real complaint; 12 (or 31 percent) went instead first to the department; 3 (or 7 percent) used some other channel. (3) The department was mentioned by 84 (or 40 percent) of all complainants in response to the first interview question; 56 (or 67 percent) of them actually went to the department; 18 (or 21 percent) went to their elected representative instead; 10 (or 12 percent) used some other channel. (4) The Ombudsman was named by 5.7 percent of all complainants as their choice in the hypothetical situation; only one (8 percent) of twelve had actually used the Ombudsman as his first channel of complaint; 5 (or 42 percent) had gone to their elected representative; 4 (or 30 percent) went to the department.

TABLE 18A

Hypothetical and Actual Complaint Behavior-- Alberta, 1971

Action in case of complaint	First complained to:				Totals	
	Ombudsman	Elected rep.	Department	All Others	N	%
Don't know--do nothing	0	15	24	15	54	25.6%
Elected rep.	0	24	12	3	39	18.5%
Department	0	18	56	10	84	39.8%
Ombudsman	1	5	4	2	12	5.7%
All others	0	6	7	9	22	10.4%
Totals N	1	68	103	39	211	
%	0.5%	32.2%	48.8%	18.5%		100.0%

TABLE 18B

Hypothetical and Actual Complaint Behavior---Britain

Action in case of complaint	First complained to:			Totals:	
	Elected rep.	Department	All Others	N	%
Don't know--do nothing	2	18	2	22	13.3%
Elected rep.	16	20	5	41	24.7%
Department	4	73	8	85	51.2%
All others	2	11	5	18	10.8%
Totals N	24	122	20	166	
%	14.5%	73.5%	12.0%		100.0%

Among British complainants we notice a somewhat different relationship between hypothetical and actual choice of channels. Some 86 percent of those who mentioned the department as their hypothetical channel, also used it for their actual complaint, but only 39 percent of those who mentioned their elected representative, actually used him for their complaint.

Table 19 presents in summary form a comparison between each sample's hypothetical and actual complaint behavior—taking all complainants as one group. A comparison between column A and B indicates how representative actual complainants are of each entire sample in terms of its hypothetical complaint behavior. Those who don't know what action to take are under-represented among actual complainants; those who would rely on the department in their hypothetical complaint behavior are over-represented among actual complainants. For the former this almost certainly means that the lack of knowledge or the lack of confidence in the process keeps them from complaining. For the latter it may mean that their confidence in the department as a complaint channel increases their willingness to make a complaint. A comparison between columns B and C shows for each sample the net switch between complainants' aggregate hypothetical and actual use of channels. We observe again a considerable difference in the complaint behavior of the Alberta and British samples. Actual use of the elected representative decreases among British complainants, while the use of the department increases sharply compared to these complainants' hypothetical use of channels. In the case of Alberta both the use of the elected representative and of the department increases.

In the earlier discussion of hypothetical complaint behavior we commented that apparently the elected representative played a more important role in grievance alleviation in the perception of the British population than in that of the Alberta or New Zealand population. In actual complaint behavior the reverse appears to be true. In the Alberta samples the hypothetical complaint behavior is a better predictor of actual behavior.

EVALUATION OF COMPLAINT EXPERIENCE

Actual complainants were also asked whether they were satisfied with the reply they received after they had appealed to their specific channel or channels. Table 20 lists the responses.

TABLE 19

Hypothetical and Actual Complaint Behavior of Sample and Complainants--Alberta and Britain

	Alberta 1969			Alberta 1971						Britain		
	A	B	C	A	B	C	A	B	C	A	B	C
Don't know--do nothing	39.4	16.6	0	39.4	25.6	0				25.9	13.3	0
Elected rep.	20.0	22.5	25.8	14.4	18.5	32.2				29.0	24.7	14.5
Department	29.3	43.7	53.0	30.6	39.8	48.8				35.5	51.2	73.5
Ombudsman	4.4	7.3	2.0	4.7	5.7	0.5				-	-	-
Others	7.2	9.9	19.2	10.7	10.4	18.5				9.6	10.8	12.0
Totals	100.3%	100%	100%	99.8%	100%	100%				100%	100%	100%

A = Sample's Hypothetical Complaint Behavior (from Table 2)

B = Complainants' Hypothetical Complaint Behavior

C = Complainants' Actual Complaint Behavior

TABLE 20

Satisfaction with Complaint Reply

	Alberta 1969	Alberta 1971	Britain 1969
Satisfied	53	46	55
Not satisfied	32	43	32
Other (incomplete)	15	11	13
Totals	100%	100%	100%
(N)	(151)	(211)	(166)

The high rate of dissatisfied complainants may surprise, but it appears as almost of constant size in all samples. Satisfaction with a complaint reply showed an unusually strong association with the respondent's attitude towards complaining. We will explore this subject in the following section.

VI. COMPLAINT BEHAVIOR AND ATTITUDES

One important question we have not raised so far is whether complaint behavior is affected by attitudes towards complaining or whether these attitudes are affected or modified by behavior, in this case, an experience with complaining. We will first examine how in our samples the decision to complain or not to complain is associated with attitudes towards complaining and political efficacy. For purposes of this discussion we are assuming that occasion or cause to complain is randomly associated with a respondent's attitudes or with his sense of political efficacy. The response predisposition of the holder of negative or critical attitudes towards complaining should be a rejection of the usefulness of complaining. The behavioral component of his negative attitude should consist of a refusal to enter into such a futile exercise. Confidence in the usefulness of complaining and the opposite belief in the futility of complaining, may therefore be expected to be important factors in separating those who do complain from those who do not. Table 21 shows that the two factors are clearly associated: relatively more of those respondents who believe complaining to be useful than of those who believe it to be futile, have, in fact, made a complaint. The tendency is—with varying strength—apparent in all three samples. However, the association of these factors is not nearly as strong as might have been expected. At least two explanations are conceivable: (1) Negative or critical attitudes towards complaining prevent some, but by no means all respondents from actually lodging their complaints; there are perhaps several other forms of behavior that are compat-

TABLE 21

Made Complaint by Attitudes Towards Complaining--
Alberta and Britain

Made Complaint		Any use in Complaining?		
		Yes	Depends	No
Alberta	Yes	18	14	11
1969[a]	No	82	86	89
Totals		100%	100%	100%
Alberta	Yes	24	19	17
1971[b]	No	76	81	83
Totals		100%	100%	100%
Britain	Yes	23	11	13
1969[c]	No	77	89	87
Totals		100%	100%	100%

a) $N = 948$ $X^2 p < .001$; Cramer's $V = .12$; Kendall's tau c = .08 (sig. .0000)
b) $N = 984$ $X^2 p = .03$; Cramer's $V = .08$; Kendall's tau c = .06 (sig. .0005)
c) $N = 930$ $X^2 p < .001$; Cramer's $V = .14$; Kendall's tau c = .10 (sig. .0000)

ible with negative attitudes towards complaining. The nature of the administrative decision or the economic and social situation of the complainant may force him to activate a complaint. (2) Since "making a complaint" would have preceded in time the reporting, in the interview, of the respondent's attitude towards complaining, we cannot rule out a change of attitudes as a result of a bad experience with complaining. Thus we may have respondents in the sample who made a complaint at a time when they had positive attitudes towards complaining; however, through the experience they acquired, and then reported in the interview, critical or negative attitudes. If there were enough respondents in this category, this might be responsible for, or it might be one factor contributing to, the possible weakening of the strong association between complaining and attitudes which we expected.

We would also expect the politically efficacious respondent to be more ready and the inefficacious to be more reluctant to make a complaint, given the nature of the political efficacy concept and the association between attitudes towards complaining and political efficacy discussed earlier. We can confirm this expectation for the 1971 Alberta sample—Table 22—but again we observe that the association of these variables is weaker than expected.[39]

TABLE 22

Made Complaint by Political Efficacy--Alberta 1971

Made Complaint?	Political Efficacy Scale[a]				
	Low 1	2	3	4	High 5
Yes	19	20	15	26	26
No	81	80	85	74	74
Totals	100%	100%	100%	100%	100%
(N)[b]	(218)	(193)	(195)	(185)	(196)

a) Scale C - see Table 12

b) N = 987; $X^2 p = 0.03$ Cramer's V = 0.10; Kendall's tau c = -.06 (sig. .001)

Again, we speculate that a low sense of political efficacy will prevent some but not all respondents with cause from registering their complaint. It is also conceivable, though less plausible,[40] that a bad complaint experience contributed to a decrease in some respondents' sense of political efficacy.

Apparently, a good proportion of those respondents, who believe complaining to be useless, or who score low on political efficacy have nevertheless made a complaint at one time or another, as can be seen from Tables 21 and 22. Since we do not know whether their reported beliefs in the futility of complaining preceded their actual complaint, we might also hypothesize that attitudes towards complaining vary significantly with whether or not a respondent has made a complaint. Table 23 presents the relationship (for one sample only) with reversed assumptions about independence of variables (compared to Table 21).

TABLE 23

Attitudes Towards Complaining by Having Made a Complaint--Alberta 1971

Any use in Complaining?	Made Complaint	
	Yes	No
Yes	59	50
Depends	21	23
No	20	27
Totals [a]	100%	100%

a) Statistics are identical with those of note (b) in Table 21

It appears that relatively more of those who had made a complaint had positive attitudes towards complaining. While that would indeed be a reassuring statement if a causal connection should be shown, the statistics cannot be used to decide which of these variables is dependent on the other, or indeed whether either or both depend on third factors.[41] Other social science research as well as our attitude concept suggest that attitudes are the primary factors, determining—to a certain extent—behavior. On the other hand, it does not appear unreasonable to suggest that an experience with complaining might modify a person's attitudes. Indeed, it appears that we can find strong evidence for this when we examine the connection between attitudes towards complaining and an evaluation of the complaint reply by complainants. Table 24 shows that complainants with a satisfactory complaint experience were much more likely to have positive attitudes towards complaining than those who had an unsatisfactory complaint experience. Three out of every four complainants with a satisfactory experience believe complaining to be useful— and that consistently in each of our three samples. The relationship

TABLE 24

Attitudes Towards Complaining by Satisfaction with Complaint Reply--Actual Complainants--Alberta and Britain

		Satisfied with Complaint Reply[d]	
Any use in Complaining?		Yes	No
Alberta 1969[a]	Yes	74	29
	Depends	15	23
	No	11	48
	Totals	100%	100%
	(N)	(80)	(44)
Alberta 1971[b]	Yes	73	34
	Depends	17	33
	No	10	33
	Totals	100%	100%
	(N)	(94)	(89)
Britain 1969[c]	Yes	75	42
	Depends	15	13
	No	10	45
	Totals	100%	100%
	(N)	(98)	(55)

a) $N = 124$; $X^2 p < .001$; Cramer's $V = .45$; Kendall's tau $c = .44$
b) $N = 183$; $X^2 p < .001$; Cramer's $V = .39$; Kendall's tau $c = .40$
c) $N = 153$; $X^2 p < .001$; Cramer's $V = .40$; Kendall's tau $c = .35$
d) "Uncertain" and "incomplete" are omitted from this table

between these two variables is such that chance and spuriousness as possible explanations must be ruled out. The only question that remains to be decided is which of the two is the independent variable, i.e., does the evaluation of a complaint experience determine a complainant's attitudes towards complaining or do his attitudes determine the way in which he appraises the experience with complaining.

The presentation in Table 24 is based on the assumption that attitudes depend on a satisfactory complaint experience. If attitudes, however, are the primary factor, we would have to postulate that the evaluation of a complaint experience is strongly influenced by a complainant's attitude towards complaining. Table 25 presents the same data with the assumptions about independence of variables reversed (in comparison with Table 24). Satisfaction with a complaint reply varies strongly with the

TABLE 25

Satisfaction with Complaint Reply by Attitudes Towards Complaining--Actual Complainants--Alberta and Britain

		Any use in Complaining?		
Satisfied with Complaint Reply?		Yes	Depends	No
Alberta	Yes	82	55	30
1969[a]	No	18	45	70
	Totals	100%	100%	100%
	(N)	(72)	(22)	(30)
Alberta	Yes	70	35	24
1971[b]	No	30	65	76
	Totals	100%	100%	100%
	(N)	(100)	(45)	(38)
Britain	Yes	76	68	29
1969[c]	No	24	32	71
	Totals	100%	100%	100%
	(N)	(96)	(22)	(35)

a) $N = 124$; $x^2 p < .001$; Cramer's V = .45; Kendall's tau c = .44
b) $N = 183$; $x^2 p < .001$; Cramer's V = .39; Kendall's tau c = .40
c) $N = 153$; $x^2 p < .001$; Cramer's V = .40; Kendall's tau c = .35

complainant's belief in the usefulness of complaining. The variation appears to be more symmetrical in Table 25 than in Table 24. Roughly three of any four complainants with positive attitudes were satisfied with their complaint experience, while again roughly three of any four complainants with negative attitudes were dissatisfied with theirs.[42]

Our surveys were not detailed enough to allow us to decide these problems on the basis of direct questions and responses. However, we tried to break down each sample into suitable smaller groups for which we then analyzed the relationship between attitudes and behavior. In this endeavor we were guided by the following expectations or hopes:

(1) if negative attitudes prevented some but not all respondents with cause from lodging their complaint we might find an indication of the reason for the different behavior;
(2) the number of respondents who may have changed their positive attitudes towards complaining after a bad complaint experience may be small relative to the entire sample. Using smaller groups for testing the association of attitudes and behavior might allow such changes to show more clearly; and
(3) if the relationship of the two variables could be clarified for those smaller groups we would gain more certainty about the same relationship in the entire sample.

TABLE 26

Attitudes Towards Complaining by Complaint Experience--
Subgroups of Respondents Scoring Lowest and Highest on
Political Efficacy Scale--Alberta 1971

Any use in Complaining?	Lowest Political Efficacy[a]		Highest Political Efficacy[b]	
	Made Complaint?		Made Complaint?	
	Yes	No	Yes	No
Yes	24	24	78	71
Depends	32	27	12	21
No	44	50	10	8
Totals	100%	100%	100%	100%
(N)	(41)	(177)	(51)	(145)

a) $N = 218$; $X^2p = .75$; Cramer's $V = 0.05$; Kendall's tau c = .02 (not sig.)
b) $N = 196$; $X^2p = .36$; Cramer's $V = 0.10$; Kendall's tau c = .04 (not sig.)

The 1971 Alberta sample showed an association between respondents' sense of political efficacy and their record of complaining (Table 22). We selected those scoring lowest and those scoring highest on a political efficacy scale [43] and compared the two groups in terms of the relative effect which complaining had on their attitudes. Table 26 shows each group separately, and we find no statistically significant association between attitudes and the fact that some had but others had not made a complaint. The two variables are independent of each other in both groups. This suggests strongly that an experience with complaining may be a minor or insignificant factor in shaping attitudes towards complaining.

Now we take from each of the two groups those who have made a complaint to see if attitudes are associated with a satisfactory complaint experience. Table 27A presents the results with the assumption that attitudes are dependent on a satisfactory complaint experience, Table 27B with the reverse assumption. Attitudes appear to be dependent on satisfaction with the complaint reply only among those of low political efficacy. There appears to be no connection between attitudes and satisfactory complaint experience among respondents with a high sense of political efficacy.

If we were correct in our earlier suggestion—that having made a complaint is not a significant factor in shaping attitudes (Table 26)—we should also consider Table 27B as the correct presentation of the relationship between complaint satisfaction and attitudes: we would conclude that among highly efficacious complainants attitudes towards complaining do not influence the evaluation of a complaint reply. Among complainants with a low sense of political efficacy the evaluation of a complaint reply is strongly influenced by the views held about the usefulness of complaining: 16 of 17 complainants in this group, who believed complaining to be useless, were dissatisfied with the reply they received. This means that they would probably report dissatisfaction with any reply they might have received. Moreover, their dissatisfaction probably serves to reinforce their prior belief about the uselessness of complaining. We are apparently dealing with people who for reasons on which we can only speculate make complaints despite a conviction that it is a futile exercise. Complaining perhaps plays the role of a self-fulfilling prophesy, confirming to the complainant the correctness of his critical views of "the system."

The political efficacy scale used in the 1971 Alberta survey is not available for the other two samples; we cannot, therefore, check whether the findings just described apply to all three samples. We can, however, choose a group of respondents—smaller than the total sample but with a high concentration of negative attitudes towards complaining—which has

TABLE 27A

Attitudes Towards Complaining by Satisfaction with Complaint Reply--Sub-groups of Respondents Scoring Lowest and Highest on Political Efficacy Scale--Alberta 1971

Any use in Complaining?	Lowest Political Efficacy[a]		Highest Political Efficacy[b]	
	Satisfied with reply?		Satisfied with reply?	
	Yes	No	Yes	No
Yes	43	16	83	75
Depends	43	32	7	17
No	14	52	10	8
Totals	100%	100%	100%	100%
(N)	(7)	(31)	(30)	(12)

a) $N = 38$; $X^2 p = .14$; Cramer's $V = .32$; Kendall's tau c $= .26$ (sig. .009)

b) $N = 42$; $X^2 p = .60$; Cramer's $V = .15$; Kendall's tau c $= .05$ (not sig.)

TABLE 27B

Satisfaction with Complaint Reply by Attitudes Towards Complaining--Sub-groups of Respondents Scoring Lowest and Highest on Political Efficacy Scale--Alberta 1971

Satisfied with Reply?	Lowest Political Efficacy[a]			Highest Political Efficacy[a]		
	Any use in Complaining?			Any use in Complaining?		
	Yes	Depends	No	Yes	Depends	No
Yes	38	23	6	74	50	75
No	62	77	94	26	50	25
Totals	100%	100%	100%	100%	100%	100%
(N)	(8)	(13)	(17)	(34)	(4)	(4)

a) Statistics are identical with those of Table 27A

TABLE 28

Attitudes Towards Complaining by Action in Case of Complaint
(Two Response Groups as Explained in Text)--Alberta and Britain

	Any use in Complaining?	Action in Case of Complaint	
		Do Nothing--Don't Know	All Others
Alberta	Yes	29	61
1969	Depends	15	23
	No	56	16
	Totals	100%	100%
Alberta	Yes	29	66
1971	Depends	25	21
	No	46	13
	Totals	100%	100%
Britain	Yes	23	57
1969	Don't know	21	23
	No	56	20
	Totals	100%	100%

identical characteristics in all three samples. We find such a group in those respondents who did not know what to do, or who would not take any action in case of complaint (in response to the first interview question). Table 28 shows that in all three samples this group of "Don't know–Do nothing" respondents was significantly less optimistic than all others about the usefulness of complaining.

We now examine this group in each sample to see whether their attitudes towards complaining vary with the fact that some had but others had not had an experience with making a complaint. Table 29 shows that attitudes in this group do not vary at a statistically significant level between respondents with and without complaint experience. Our group had a higher concentration of negative attitudes towards complaining. Yet

[54]

we find no statistically significant difference in attitudes between those who had experience with complaining and those who had none. This again strongly suggests that a change of attitudes as a result of a bad complaint experience is a minor or insignificant factor in shaping attitudes.

TABLE 29

Attitudes Towards Complaining by Complaint Experience--
Sub-group of "Do nothing--don't know" Respondents of
First Interview Question

		Made Complaint?	
Any use in Complaining?		Yes	No
Alberta	Yes	36	28
1969[a]	Depends	0	17
	No	64	55
	Totals	100%	100%
	(N)	(22)	(336)
Alberta	Yes	30	27
1971[b]	Depends	28	30
	No	42	43
	Totals	100%	100%
	(N)	(53)	(334)
Britain	Yes	33	22
1969[c]	Don't know	10	22
	No	57	56
	Totals	100%	100%
	(N)	(21)	(216)

a) $N = 358$; $X^2 p = .11$; Cramer's $V = 0.11$; Kendall's tau $c = .005$ (not sig.)
b) $N = 387$; $X^2 p = .88$; Cramer's $V = 0.02$; Kendall's tau $c = .01$ (not sig.)
c) $N = 237$; $X^2 p = .08$; Cramer's $V = 0.12$; Kendall's tau $c = .04$ (sig. .08)

Yet when we examine the possible effect of an unsatisfactory complaint reply on the attitudes of the few in this group who did make a complaint we find the same extremely strong association of these two variables in each of our three samples: Table 30A presents the data with the assumption that attitudes depend on satisfaction with complaining and Table 30B with the reverse assumption.

If we were correct in the earlier conclusion—that attitudes do not vary in our group between those with and those without complaint experience—we

TABLE 30A

Attitudes Towards Complaining by Satisfaction with Complaint Reply--Actual Complainants of "Don't know--Do nothing" Group of Respondents--Alberta and Britain

		Satisfied with Complaint Reply?			
		Yes		No	
Any use in Complaining?		(N)	%	(N)	%
Alberta 1969[a]	Yes	(4)	80	(3)	19
	Depends	–	–	–	–
	No	(1)	20	(13)	81
	Totals	(5)	100%	(16)	100%
Alberta 1971[b]	Yes	(6)	37	(7)	21
	Depends	(7)	44	(8)	24
	No	(3)	19	(18)	55
	Totals	(16)	100%	33	100%
Britain 1969[c]	Yes	(6)	67	(1)	8
	Depends	(2)	22	(0)	0
	No	(1)	11	(11)	92
	Totals	(9)	100%	(12)	100%

a) $N = 21$; $X^2_p = .04$; Phi $= .55$; Kendall's tau b $= .55$ (sig. .0002)
b) $N = 49$; $X^2_p = .05$; Cramer's V $= .33$; Kendall's tau c $= .31$ (sig. .0007)
c) $N = 21$; $X^2_p = .001$; Cramer's V $= .80$; Kendall's tau c $= .77$ (sig. .0000)

must also accept that the type of complaint experience which respondents reported is not the factor determining his attitudes. But since a strong association between attitudes and complaint evaluation exists, both among all complainants, and—more strongly even—among complainants in this group, we must accept that it is a complainant's attitude which determines the way in which he evaluates his complaint experience. Some 86 to 93 percent of those in our groups with negative attitudes towards complaining reported an unsatisfactory complaint experience; some 46 to 86 percent of those with positive attitudes reported a satisfactory complaint experience.

TABLE 30B

Satisfaction with Complaint Reply by Attitudes Towards Complaining--Actual Complainants of "Don't know--Do nothing" Group of Respondents--Alberta and Britain

		Any use in Complaining?					
		Yes		Depends		No	
Satisfied with Reply?		(N)	%	(N)	%	(N)	%
Alberta	Yes	(4)	57	-	-	(1)	7
1969[a]	No	(3)	43	-	-	(13)	93
	Totals	(7)	100%	-	-	(14)	100%
Alberta	Yes	(6)	46	(7)	47	(3)	14
1971[b]	No	(7)	54	(8)	53	(18)	86
	Totals	(13)	100%	(15)	100%	(21)	100%
Britain	Yes	(6)	86	(2)	100	(1)	8
1969[c]	No	(1)	14	(0)	0	(11)	92
	Totals	(7)	100%	(2)	100%	(12)	100%

a) $N = 21$; $x^2 p = .04$; Phi = .55; Kendall's tau b = .55 (sig. .0002)

b) $N = 49$; $x^2 p = .05$; Cramer's V = .33; Kendall's tau c = .31 (sig. .0007)

c) $N = 21$; $x^2 p = .001$; Cramer's V = .80; Kendall's tau c = .77 (sig. .0000)

The possibility that we have in our sample respondents who underwent attitude changes—from positive to negative—as a result of an experience with complaining are extremely small. We may therefore discard the second speculative explanation of the relatively weak association between attitudes and the decision to complain.[44] The first speculation now appears as the more plausible explanation of the relationship between attitudes and complaint behavior: our expectation is confirmed in that negative attitudes towards complaining prevent some people from complaining. However, the majority of people with negative attitudes are likely to lodge a complaint anyway and then to evaluate their complaint experience as unsatisfactory.

VII. CONCLUSIONS

We have examined the hypothetical complaint behavior of two samples of the Alberta population and of one sample of the British population. A surprisingly large proportion of each sample appeared determined not to take any action in case of perceived maladministration, and an even larger proportion was at a loss to indicate what action they might take. Significantly more Albertans were found in these groups than British respondents. We conclude that the traditional formal as well as informal channels of complaining do not play an important role in these respondents' perception of their political environment. But we also discovered that their apparent ignorance and even their expressed determination not to take any action, did, in fact, not prevent some of them—at least in the past—from raising a complaint.

Some of the formal avenues of appeal, especially legal recourse, were found to play a much less significant role than has traditionally been attributed to them in constitutional writings. Political and administrative avenues of complaining share about equally the task of grievance alleviation in the perception of both populations. It first appeared that elected representatives played a more important role for the British population than for the Alberta population. A later examination of the actual use of channels indicated that elected representatives may in fact be used more frequently as a first avenue of appeal by the Alberta population. It also appeared later that a greater proportion of the Alberta sample than of the British attributed the highest effectiveness to the elected representative as a channel of complaint. It was interesting to observe that a strikingly similar proportion of each population (about one third) would use administrative channels to air their complaint, although only about one fifth of each sample attributed a high effectiveness to this recourse. When we considered the choice of channels among those who had made a complaint we found that one half (Alberta) and three quarters (Britain) of complainants first sought a remedy by appealing to the administrative agency which caused the problem. This suggests that complainants in our samples distinguish relatively clearly between the propriety of using a particular channel first and their expectation that a specific channel will be effective in producing the results desired. The news media do not loom very high in either population's awareness of channels of complaint, and are used relatively rarely by those who had complaint experience. However, an astonishingly high proportion of each population, in particular of the British sample, attributed effectiveness to the news media.

Our respondents' sense of political efficacy was found to be the most important variable associated with both their awareness of channels and the effectiveness attributed to channels of complaint. The level of educational attainment was the second most important explanatory factor for each sample's hypothetical complaint behavior, though not of the effectiveness which was attributed to channels. Respondents' socio-economic status played a significant secondary role in explaining the hypothetical complaint behavior, the effectiveness attributed to channels, and—for the Alberta samples at least—of the actual complaint behavior. For the British sample socio-economic status was the primary factor, education a secondary, in explaining actual complaint behavior.

The incidence of complaining was found to be surprisingly low in each sample; we may be dealing here with a more general phenomenon. It appears that four fifths of each population have not complained. As mentioned above, education and socio-economic factors are influential in respondents' decision to complain. The incidence of complaining increases with increasing levels of education and socio-economic status.

It is worth considering the proposition that more complaining should be encouraged, preferably, of course, the right kind of complaining and in the most appropriate manner. The system quite probably deserves more complaining, i.e., more errors than complaints occur. And complaining, potentially, has therapeutic effects on both the individual who complains and the administrator who erred, and perhaps even on the politician who was instrumental in rectifying the error. These effects deserve more attention and study. If they are found to exist, we may be able to attempt changes in attitudes towards complaining: both administrators and complainants might consider complaining less of a nuisance, a waste of time, or deviant behavior, and more as just another rational way of ensuring the proper functioning of the administrative system. The Alberta data suggest that we may expect for the future an increase in the proportion of a population who will complain. Any increase will, however, not be a dramatic one because attitudes and political efficacy perceptions, which influence the decision to complain, are not likely to change radically or speedily. The only prospect for an acceleration of attitude changes arises from the strong association between attitudes and education: the explosion of educational opportunities may bring about some noticeable changes within a five- to ten-year period.

We found positive attitudes towards complaining with under one half of each sample, sceptical attitudes with one fifth, and negative attitudes with a little over one quarter of each sample. The distribution of attitudes towards complaining was strikingly similar in all three samples.

Political attitudes are acquired through the process of political socialization. Attitudes towards complaining are not different; they are part of an individual's belief system, of which we measured one part with our "sense of political efficacy" scale in one sample. The question about the usefulness of complaining in a way measures broadly the same phenomenon, and it was found useful to include it in the base of the political efficacy scale. Sense of political efficacy and, separately, attitudes towards complaining were found to be strongly dependent on respondents' level of education and socio-economic status. We were able to show that it is attitudes that determine behavior in complaining, and not the reverse: experience with complaining has no apparent impact on attitudes. In fact, the opposite appears to be true, at least for part of the sample. It was found that among complainants with a low sense of political efficacy, negative attitudes towards complaining strongly influenced their perception of the complaint experience. In each sample we found a group of people who complained—despite their belief that it is useless—and who were almost all dissatisfied with the reply they received. We are dealing perhaps with 1 or 2 percent of the population and 5 percent of actual complainants. The therapeutic value of complaining apparently is lost completely on this group.

The worst consequences of these findings would be that people at a low socio-economic level and with little education are socialized to have negative attitudes towards complaining; they have a low sense of political efficacy and, as a result, are more reluctant to make a complaint. Their failure to complain probably reinforces their sceptical or negative attitudes towards complaining and their belief in their own inability to effect a change. Even if they do complain, their expectations about the uselessness of complaining will often lead them to be dissatisfied with the result of an investigation. One would normally expect a gradual change in this situation through increasing standards of living and more education. The

[60]

Ombudsman in one sense represents an effort to short-circuit this lengthy route of social improvement, to break out of the vicious circle just described by offering a simple, easily accessible, and politically independent appeal channel. Given the nature of attitudes and the influence of education and socio-economic status as well as attitudes on behavior it remains to be seen whether the short circuit will produce significant results. Our findings suggest that the Ombudsman is likely to have a number of unsatisfiable clients. It will take a considerable effort on his part, and the utilization of all his resources and skills to convert some of them.

NOTES

1. Gellhorn's book (1966) is an obvious exception. The increasing literature on Ombudsmen is paying some attention to the subject of complaining although most of the writers concern themselves with the development of the institution. Because it is difficult to get access to data about complainants there is a paucity of empirical studies—with one exception: L. B. Hill's (1970) study of the New Zealand Ombudsman offers a detailed examination of the Ombudsman's complainants based on a content analysis of a sample of the Ombudsman's files. (This section also published separately: Hill, 1971.)

2. For an excellent account of the earliest beginnings see Barrow, 1956: chap. XVII. Also, Jolliffe, 1961: Part IV and V.

3. When Alberta's political leaders considered the establishment of an Ombudsman in 1966 they were thoroughly convinced that there would not be a significant number of complaints in the province. Yet the Ombudsman receives some 800 complaints annually and members of the Provincial Legislature report that their own mailbags have not become smaller since the Ombudsman began his work in 1967. On the other side of the Atlantic, British MPs, in a debate on the need for an Ombudsman, estimated that they receive some 300,000 complaints annually from constituents. (Great Britain, *House of Commons Debates,* Vol. 640, cc. 1693-1756.) When the Parliamentary Commissioner (British Ombudsman) was appointed in 1967 he predicted a flow of 7,000 complaints annually from MPs to himself on behalf of citizens yet he has received fewer than 1,000 requests per year and the numbers have declined over the years. The figures given by the P.C.A. in his Annual Report are: 743 (1967), 808 (1968), 814 (1969), 645 (1970), 548 (1971), 573 (1972), 571 (1973).

4. For a short description of the sampling plans see Appendix A.

5. On a comparative basis Almond and Verba, 1963.

6. The development of the political efficacy scale is discussed separately below in section IV.

7. As asked in the 1971 Alberta survey. The question was asked with a slight variation in the U.K. survey: "If you had a complaint about a civil servant or a government agency who had treated you unfairly, what do you think you would do about it?"

8. Approximately 3 to 6 percent of respondents offered a third response and some 1 to 2 percent a fourth response.

9. From interviewer reports it was apparent that there were several elements involved in the attitude underlying this response. One was peculiar to Canada. Several responses of this type were reported: "I am grateful to be in Canada. I wouldn't complain even if I were treated unfairly." The 1971 Alberta survey confirmed that ethnicity and nativity do influence the readiness to complain (assuming that occasion to complain is randomly associated with country of birth and ethnic background of respondents). Of those born outside Canada (N = 222) 19.4 percent had actually made a complaint (the figure for the entire sample is 21 percent); respondents born in the British Isles, the Netherlands and Russia had a higher proportion of complainants (25-27 percent); those born in Germany and the U.S. had an average rate (19 percent); those from the rest of Europe and other countries a very low rate (8 percent). Of the same sample (Alberta 1971) 94 percent reported their ethnic background. While 21.5 percent of these 938 respondents had made a complaint, we find some groups with a higher rate (Anglo-Saxon 23.3 percent, German 23 percent, Scandinavian 24.2 percent, Dutch 26.9 percent) and others with a lower rate of complaining (Russian-Ukrainian 17.2 percent, French 11.4 percent, Polish 9.4 percent, other European 14.5 percent, native Indians 12.5 percent).

10. For details see Table 14.

11. Some 16 percent (Alberta 1971) and 13 percent (U.K.) of the "Do nothing" –respondents had made a complaint.

12. Mitchell, 1968: 22. The figures in our Table 2 were reconstructed from the somewhat loosely reported responses in Mitchell's Table 2.

13. Cramer's V ranges from 0 to 1 regardless of the size of the table being tested. For a 2 x 2 table Cramer's V will be equal to phi (phi makes a correction for the fact that the value of chi-square is directly proportional to that of N by adjusting the X^2 value).

14. This variable is explained below, pp. 28-32.

15. Two different scales for measuring education were used. In Alberta we ascertained the type of schooling completed by a respondent. In the U.K. two measures were tried: (1) at which age the respondent completed his education, and (2) whether or not the respondent had "further education after school." In the text we will refer (for the U.K. only) to the first measure as "Education (1)" and the second as "Education (2)."

16. Interviewers were instructed to assess the respondent's socio-economic level on a five-point scale ranging from "Much below average" to "Much above average." This measure is obviously a little crude in that it is not very precise and potentially influenced by varying interviewer values. The justification for its use is that it is one common measure for the total sample (while income or occupation never describes the entire sample).

17. The following values were obtained for Cramer's V:

	Alberta (1971)	Britain
Political efficacy	.22	.20
Education (2)	.17	.17
Occupation	.15	.16
Socio-economic level	.14	.14
Income	.12	.14

Other variables also indicated a statistically significant association: age, sex and an urbanization scale. Age and sex, however, lost their significance in both samples when partial correlations were computed controlling for the effects of education or socio-economic level.

18. "Sense of political efficacy" scale for the 1971 Alberta survey is a six-point scale trichotomized, based on five scale items: Scale B in Table 12 below.

19. The Political Efficacy scale used in the British survey is a four-point scale based on three scale items. See also note 30.

20. The statistical assumptions for partialling are not met by nominal data (hypothetical complaint behavior); however, most of the other variables are ordinal. Two further precautions used are: (1) associations were accepted as statistically significant only at the .001 level and (2) our conclusions were limited to statements of the relative importance of several independent variables.

21. To the extent that "sense of political efficacy" is itself associated with education and socio-economic variables, we suspect that it covaries with hypothetical complaint behavior, although the values of the partial correlation coefficients decreased only slightly when we controlled for education; e.g., the value of the Zero Order Partial for hypothetical complaint behavior and political efficacy was for Alberta, 1971: .20. When controlled for education the value was .17 and still significant at the .001 level. For the British survey the variation in the value of the Partial correlation coefficient was even less.

22. Except for obvious institutional differences the list contained the same channels for all samples. The Ombudsman was deliberately left out of this list, because several later questions in these interviews were employed to probe respondents' knowledge of the Ombudsman in depth.

23. The N for each sample is: 1010 for Alberta 1969, 994 for Alberta 1971, and 1000 for Britain. In this and subsequent tables the N will be given only if it deviates from the N of the respective total sample.

24. The British survey contained two additional questions asking specifically whether in the opinion of the respondents MPs were doing a good job in dealing with constituents' complaints, and whether councillors were doing a good job with local complaint. Detailed analysis (to be reported elsewhere) showed that the rating given to councillors was appreciably and consistently better than that given to MPs.

25. According to a survey of MPs taken in 1968 and reported in Friedmann, 1970: 232-259.

26. In both the 1971 Alberta sample and the British sample the socio-economic variables diminish somewhat in importance when we control for the effects of education either through control tables or through Partial correlations.

27. For details of the scale see Table 11 and 12.

28. The scale was developed and published first by Campbell, et al., 1954: 187-189. For a listing of the scale see Robinson, 1969: 459-460. For a discussion of all efforts see Mokken, 1969: 427-429.

29. R should be at least .90 and S should be .60 or better for Guttman scales.

30. The statistics indicate that it is probably not unidimensional. The 1969 Alberta survey and the British survey contained two individual political efficacy items (items 4 and 7 of Table 11). A political efficacy scale was created based on those two items and the question on usefulness of complaining. It is a scale with low reliability and is used here only occasionally as a cumulative scale (Table 7).

31. L. B. Hill (1970: chap. VIII) took a thorough look at the potential for complaints arising out of the normal work of all New Zealand government departments and concluded that with all the potential for conflict the small number of actual complaints had to be considered as surprising.

32. The number of respondents who have actually lodged a complaint is considerably smaller than the proportion of respondents in the Almond and Verba study (1963: 184-187) who said that they were likely to take action to change some regulation.

33. A further and similar problem has to be seen in how the respondent interprets the nature of a complaint. He may feel he has only a "question," but it may be a very real complaint. Hill's (1970) content analysis of New Zealand Ombudsman cases revealed that such a perception (or posture of modesty?) occurs surprisingly frequently.

34. Kendall's tau c can also be used, and confirms the differential strength of association for the British sample as indicated earlier by Cramer's V. Kendall's tau c:

Occupation	.10
Income	.12
Socio-econ. level	.12
Education (1)	.09

All are significant at the .0000 level. (Occupation in this case does not include housewives. The three categories: Manual, Clerical, Professional can be treated as ordinal data.)

35. In the British sample: men 20 percent, women 14 percent; Alberta 1969: men 17 percent, women 13 percent; Alberta 1971: men 25 percent, women 18 percent. Hill (1971: 5) reports also that more men than women were among the New Zealand Ombudsman's clients.

36. For this cross-tabulation: $X^2 p < .01$ and Cramer's V = .10.

37. Kendall's tau c = .20; Significance .0002.

38. The 1969 Alberta sample is not tabulated but shows a pattern almost identical with that of the 1971 sample.

39. The two individual political efficacy items in the British survey do not show a statistically significant association with making a complaint: the tendency for the more efficacious to complain more is visible, but it is not statistically significant.

40. Less plausible, because "sense of political efficacy" was measured indirectly through a scale, while attitudes to complaining were recorded in response to one direct question.

41. Ideally one would interview a larger sample of each population to have a larger number of respondents with complaint experience. One would then conduct in depth interviews with them concerning their attitudes before and after their complaint experiences.

42. Both Cramer's V and Kendall's tau c are based on frequency distributions and are, of course, identical for each sample in the two tables.

43. These are the respondents represented in Columns 1 and 5 of Table 22. The political efficacy scale used in that table does not contain the item on usefulness of complaining. It is Scale C as identified in Table 12.

44. Above, pp. 45-46.

REFERENCES

ALMOND, G. A. and S. VERBA (1963) The Civic Culture. Political Attitudes and Democracy in Five Nations. Princeton: Princeton Univ. Press.

BARROW, G. W. S. (1956) Feudal Britain. London: Edward Arnold.

CAMPBELL, A., G. GURIN, W. E. MILLER (1954) The Voter Decides. Evanston, Ill.: Row, Peterson.
FRIEDMANN, K. A. (1970) Kontrolle der Verwaltung in England. Meisenheim: Verlag Anton Hain.
GELLHORN, W. (1966) When Americans Complain. Cambridge: Harvard Univ. Press.
HILL, L. B. (1971) "Socio-psychological dimensions of complaints to Ombudsmen: a New Zealand analysis." The 67th Meeting of The American Political Science Association, Chicago, 1971.
——— (1970) The International Transfer of Political Institutions: A Behavioral Analysis of the New Zealand Ombudsman. Unpublished Dissertation: Tulane University, New Orleans.
JOLLIFFE, J. E. A. (1961) The Constitutional History of Medieval England. London: Adam and Charles Black.
MITCHELL, A. (1968) "The people and the system: some basic attitudes." New Zealand Journal of Public Administration (1968) 19-35.
MOKKEN, R. K. (1968/1969) "Dutch-American comparisons of the 'sense of political efficacy': some remarks on cross-cultural 'robustness'," Acta Politica 4 (1969) 425-448.
ROBINSON, J. P., J. G. RUSK and K. B. HEAD (1969) Measures of Political Attitudes. Ann Arbor: Survey Research Center.
ROKEACH, M. (1968) "The nature of attitudes." International Encyclopedia of the Social Sciences, Vol. I: 449-457.
SHAW, M. E. and J. M. WRIGHT (1967) Scales for the Measurement of Attitudes. New York: McGraw-Hill.

APPENDIX

SAMPLING PLANS AND SURVEY ADMINISTRATION

(1) ALBERTA

The main purpose of the surveys was to study public knowledge of and attitudes towards the Alberta Ombudsman. Hypothetical and actual complaint behavior and attitudes towards complaining were subsidiary objects of study. It appeared necessary to take into account the highly diverse environments within Alberta, ranging from the two large cities of Calgary and Edmonton to rural communities of a few hundred people. It was therefore decided to stratify the sample on the basis of urbanization. According to the 1966 Census data (Dominion Bureau of Statistics, Census of Canada 1966, "Population: Rural and Urban Distribution," March 1968, pp. 92-608) the following categories appeared necessary:

	Percentage of Population of Alberta in 1966 Census
1. Metropolitan areas (Calgary, Edmonton)	52%
2. Cities between 20,000 and 40,000 (Medicine Hat, Lethbridge, Red Deer)	6%
3. Towns between 1,000 and 20,000	11%
4. Villages less than 1,000	12%
5. Residents on farms and ranches	19%

Since only the metropolitan areas of Alberta, as in the rest of Canada, are divided into census tracts, it was not possible to adopt a uniform sampling plan within each subpopulation. The following sampling plans were devised, which in each case were determined by (a) the available knowledge about a stratum and (b) the resources available for carrying out the interviewing:

1. The metropolitan subpopulation was further stratified into the two cities of Calgary and Edmonton, for both of which census tracts are defined. Since data on the percentage of home ownership within each tract are also available, it was decided to divide the tracts into three groups within each city, according to whether or not they fall into the upper, middle, or lower third on this basis. Home ownership is not perfectly correlated with income, but it is certainly related, and it is in this case the only aggregate statistic available by which to differentiate the tracts. Such a stratification at least improved the chances that the interviewer would meet a number of the less well-to-do people, thus reducing the middle-class bias often found in surveys of this type.

    Within each city, then, 10 census tracts were randomly selected, three from the upper third, four from the middle third, and three from the lower third. (Dominion Bureau of Statistics, Census of Canada 1966. "Population: Edmonton," August 1968, 95-626; "Population: Calgary," August 1968, 95-625.)

    Finally within each census tract, two intersections were randomly selected from which the interviewers collected twelve or thirteen interviews. Appropriate maps were not available to design a true cluster sample (i.e., to randomly select blocks of houses), so in the last analysis this sampling plan has the characteristics of a quota sample; but as many safeguards as possible against the bias of the interviewers were built in. It was not felt that the extra time and expense necessary to produce a true multi-stage cluster sample of Calgary and Edmonton would be a reasonable investment, since quota sampling is unavoidable in any case for the rural parts of the province.

2. The stratum of the population living in places numbering 20,000-40,000 people was divided into three substrata consisting of the three cities of Red Deer, Medicine Hat, and Lethbridge. Although census tracts are not available, two intersections were randomly selected from a city map and an interviewer sent to each to collect 15 interviews apiece.

3. The towns of 1,000-20,000 inhabitants were enumerated (excluding the far north, which at that time of the year, February, it was not practical to survey) and three were randomly chosen. A quota of 40 interviews was collected from each.

4. It would have been desirable to choose a number of villages at random in the province, but our resources did not permit such a dispersion of the interviewing teams. It was necessary therefore to select villages in the wider vicinity of the three larger cities (Red Deer, Medicine Hat, Lethbridge). The villages in each area were listed and a choice of one per region randomly made. A quota of 50 interviews was collected from each.

5. Associated with the teams being sent to the various cities, towns and villages were interviewers who drove to the surrounding countryside to collect a total of 150 interviews from farm and ranch families.

As projected the composition of the sample was as follows:

Stratum	Number	Percent	Population Percent
Metropolitan	500	50	52
Cities	90	9	6
Towns	120	12	11
Villages	150	15	12
Farms	150	15	19

The sample was thus very close to proportionate.

The sampling plan was identical for the 1969 and the 1971 surveys; where a random choice of census tract, town or village was necessary, a new choice was, of course, made for the 1971 survey.

(2) BRITAIN

The survey of the British population was carried out in May 1969.

The sample was stratified on the basis of urbanization. According to the "Sample Census 1966, Great Britain, Summary Tables," and the Registrar General's "Annual Estimates of the Population of England and Wales and of Local Authority Area—1968" the following plan appeared necessary, and was completed:

Stratum	Percentage of Population	Planned Interviews	Percentage of Sample	Percentage of Interviews Completed
1. Conurbations	34.1	350	35	34
2. Urban areas over 100,000	13.5	150	15	15
3. Urban areas with 50,000-100,000	9.8	100	10	10
4. Urban areas with pop. under 50,000	21.5	200	20	20.1
5. Rural districts	21.1	200	20	20.9

A uniform sampling plan was adopted for the first four categories. Within each category all relevant cities were enumerated and a random choice made accordingly:

1. Three conurbations were randomly chosen (from seven): Greater London (150 interviews), South-East Lancashire (Manchester) and Clydeside (Glasgow) (100 interviews each).
2. Urban areas over 100,000 population: two were randomly chosen for 75 interviews each (Ipswich and Reading).
3. Urban areas with 50,000 to 100,000 inhabitants: two were randomly chosen for 50 interviews each (Gillingham and Worcester).
4. Urban areas under 50,000 inhabitants: four were randomly chosen for 50 interviews each (Kempston, Witney, Hitchin, Kettering).

Tenure of housing provides an excellent guide to income and socio-economic status in Britain. Very detailed data on "Dwellings by Tenure" were available for the

1966 Sample Census; the Ministry of Housing and Local Government kindly allowed access to its microfilm collection of these data in London (for England and Wales) and Edinburgh (for Clydeside):

1. Each of the 3 conurbations chosen was subdivided into three groups of boroughs: (1) those with a high density of owner-occupiers; (2) those with a high density of privately rented dwellings; and (3) those with a high density of council rented dwellings. Two boroughs were randomly chosen from each group. The boroughs were further subdivided into census districts along the same line of high density owner-occupier, privately rented and council rented dwellings. For each category two appropriate census districts were then randomly chosen, and two intersections in each designated for collection of a quota of interviews.

2.- The same procedure (as for conurbations) was applied to strata 2 to 4, except
4. that only one breakdown per city was carried out.

5. Villages within the wider vicinity of each of the cities (strata 2 to 4) were enumerated, and a choice of one per region randomly made for a collection of a quota of 25 interviews and total of 200 interviews.

KARL FRIEDMANN is presently Associate Professor of Political Science at The University of Calgary, Alberta, Canada. He received his Ph.D. from the University of Heidelberg, and is the author of a book (in German) on Parliamentary control of public administration in Britain, and several journal articles. He is currently preparing for publication a book on the Alberta Ombudsman.